T0318701

Cambridge Elements ≡

Elements in Evolutionary Economics
edited by
John Foster
University of Queensland
Jason Potts
RMIT University

A RECONSIDERATION OF THE THEORY OF NON-LINEAR SCALE EFFECTS

The Sources of Varying Returns to, and Economies of, Scale

Richard G. Lipsey
Simon Fraser University, British Columbia

CAMBRIDGE
UNIVERSITY PRESS

CAMBRIDGE
UNIVERSITY PRESS

University Printing House, Cambridge CB2 8BS, United Kingdom

One Liberty Plaza, 20th Floor, New York, NY 10006, USA

477 Williamstown Road, Port Melbourne, VIC 3207, Australia

314–321, 3rd Floor, Plot 3, Splendor Forum, Jasola District Centre, New Delhi – 110025, India

79 Anson Road, #06–04/06, Singapore 079906

Cambridge University Press is part of the University of Cambridge.

It furthers the University's mission by disseminating knowledge in the pursuit of education, learning, and research at the highest international levels of excellence.

www.cambridge.org
Information on this title: www.cambridge.org/9781108453097
DOI: 10.1017/9781108555029

© Richard G. Lipsey 2018

This publication is in copyright. Subject to statutory exception and to the provisions of relevant collective licensing agreements, no reproduction of any part may take place without the written permission of Cambridge University Press.

First published 2018

A catalogue record for this publication is available from the British Library.

ISBN 978-1-108-45309-7 Paperback
ISSN 2514-3573 (online)
ISSN 2514-3581 (print)

Cambridge University Press has no responsibility for the persistence or accuracy of URLs for external or third-party internet websites referred to in this publication and does not guarantee that any content on such websites is, or will remain, accurate or appropriate.

A Reconsideration of the Theory of Non-Linear Scale Effects

Richard G. Lipsey

Abstract: *The main thrust of this Element is a critical assessment of the theory and evidence concerning the sources of scale effects. It is argued that the analysis of static scale effects is important because scale effects are embedding in our world, and new technologies associated with an evolving economy often allow their exploitation when they cannot be exploited in less technically advanced and smaller economies. So, although static equilibrium theory is not a good vehicle for studying economic growth, showing how scale effects operate when output varies with given technology helps us to understand the scale effects that occur when output rises as a result of economic growth, even though that is typically driven by technological change.*

The set of production functions that are consistent with Viner's treatment of long-run cost curves are distinguished from the single production function that is found in virtually all modern microeconomic textbooks. It is argued that the inconsistencies and ambiguities relating to the use of such a single production function to cover all possible scales of a firm's operations are such that it is an imperfect tool for analysing the scale effects that firms actually face. The relation between scale effects and the size of the firm are discussed. It is shown that under certain commonly occurring circumstances the ability to replicate production facilities is consistent with short ranges of diseconomies of scale and an indefinite range of increasing returns.

Next comes a detailed analysis of the sources of positive scale effects and a critical assessment of the treatment of these in a large sample of

I am indebted to Kenneth Carlaw, Curtis Eaton and Colin McLean for comments and suggestions, and also to Colin McLean for his indefatigable research efforts.

the existing literature. It is argued that the nature of our world, with its three dimensions, its physical laws and the many random elements in its behaviour, is such that when the scale of anything changes, we should always expect to encounter non-linear scale effects. Most authors list a series of examples of sources that are assumed to give rise to scale effects but seldom attempt to show in any detail how these are supposed to work. When we do this, some alleged sources are found not to give rise to scale effects at all, while others have effects that differ from what has been assumed. Furthermore, there is seldom agreement among authors as to whether a particular source is a cause of varying returns to scale or economies of scale. Most authors argue that indivisibilities are an important source of scale effects, although these are seldom well defined, nor are the precise ways in which these are supposed to work typically analysed. When we do this, we identify two basic types of indivisibilities, ex post and ex ante, plus several variations of each of these main types. We then argue that the discussion of indivisibilities has been confused by use of different implicit definitions of the term and also that only one of these types of indivisibility can be a source of scale effects. Constant-returns production functions are found to be inconsistent with much that is known about actual production techniques, even when firms expand by duplicating identical plants. Unless ruled out by definition, diseconomies of scale are found to be a real possibility in many circumstances. When these occur in some parts of complex capital goods or plants, they limit the extent to which economies in other parts can be exploited by increasing the scale of the whole operation. Finally, brief consideration is given to the literature concerning the factors that limit the exploitation of the scale effects that are ubiquitous in the real world and to the consequences of their exploitation.

Keywords: economies of scale, production function, returns to scale, indivisibilities, replication, long-run cost curves.

JEL Classification: D 240

ISBNs: 9781108555029 (OC), 9781108453097 (PB)

ISSNs: 2514-3573 (online), 2514-3581 (print)

We live in a three-dimensional world subject to both physical laws and uncertainty. These cause ubiquitous scale effects related to the world's geometry, its physics and the random aspects of its behaviour. We define these effects generically as anything that affects the firm as a result of changing its scale of operations. When new firms or industries are developed, old ones are expanded or new technologies are developed, scale effects are typically encountered. Even when these are fully exploited in equilibrium, their existence affects the approach to and the nature of that equilibrium. All of these scale effects are typical of growing economies, and they interact with economic growth in a relation of mutual causation. (Different types of scale effects are distinguished later in the Element, and since the Element contains a large number of terms, some of which are novel, they are listed along with their definitions in Appendix A.)

Here are three relevant questions about scale effects: (i) What are the sources of such effects? (ii) What conditions lead to their being exploited? (iii) What are the consequences of the common existence of scale effects? The purpose of this Element is to consider in detail the first question, although that inevitably overlaps to some extent with the second question, which will be considered briefly near the end of this Element but with no pretence at completeness. The important question (iii) is already the subject of extensive literature and so is only considered briefly near the end of this Element.

Most of the analysis in microtheory textbooks is conducted assuming a constant-returns-to-scale production function because the non-convexities introduced by scale effects are analytically much more difficult to handle than the convexities of constant returns. Indeed, when an aggregate production function is used with labour and capital as the main inputs, scale effects pose aggregation problems that are intractable for all practical purposes. As a result, scale effects tend to be treated as exceptions rather than what they actually are: the rule to which constant returns are the exception. Also, most of the treatments in micro textbooks are highly abstract and readers are seldom asked to give examples of what some formal result would look like in terms of real-world examples.

Indeed, few authors attempt to show how the sources they list are supposed to operate in any detail. When we do this, some of the alleged sources are found to have different effects from what have been assumed, and others are found not to cause scale effects at all. Furthermore, many authors argue that indivisibilities are an important source of scale effects, although there is no agreement as to how these should be defined, nor are the precise ways in which these are supposed to work typically modelled in any formal way. When we do these things, we find many confusions and mistaken conclusions in the existing literature on indivisibilities.

In preparing the Element, I surveyed entries related to the sources of scale effects in all economic encyclopaedias and dictionaries of economics that I could locate. I also surveyed a selection of microeconomics textbooks aimed at various levels and some relevant articles. I stopped covering textbooks when I felt I had enough to illustrate the treatment of scale effects in the literature so that little would be gained by surveying more. In Section 2, I investigate the working of some of these alleged sources both to check on their validity as sources and to illustrate, without any attempt to be exhaustive, the unexplored complexity of the effects associated with some of the alleged sources.

After some preliminary ground clearing, the Element discusses the representation of scale effects through the firm's cost and production functions. A treatment of the sources of scale effects, particularly in the reconfiguration of capital goods, leads to a distinction between the set of production functions that are consistent with the Viner treatment of the long-run cost curves and the unique production function that is found in virtually all modern micro textbooks. Problems related to the concept of a production function that spans the whole of input space are first discussed in the text and then elaborated in Appendix B. After that, the relation between scale effects and firm size is discussed. Most of the rest of the Element provides a critical assessment of, and an elaboration on, the treatment of the sources of scale effects in the literature. It argues that the nature of our world is such that when the scale of almost anything is changed, we should expect to encounter scale effects. Surprises should only occur when such effects are not encountered. A major section on the confusion over the meaning of indivisibilities, and the manner in which they do and do not cause scale effects, is followed by a treatment of the sources of scale effects that are associated with the design of capital goods. Finally, brief consideration is given to the literature concerning the factors that limit the exploitation of the scale effects that are ubiquitous in the real world and to the consequences of their exploitation.

1 Background Conceptual Issues

1.1 The Use of Static Analysis

Most of the study of the sources of scale effects in the literature is done by comparing equilibrium situations in static models assuming given technological possibilities. Although many in the scale effects are associated with economic growth, much can be learned from the study of scale effects using comparative statics, which we do at some length in this Element. The analysis of static scale effects is useful because scale effects are embedded in our world, and new technologies associated with an evolving economy often allow their exploitation when they cannot be exploited in less technically advanced and smaller economies. Although static equilibrium theory is not a good vehicle for studying economic growth, it can be used effectively to study both the nature and sources of these scale effects. By showing how and why they occur when output varies with present technology, we can better understand the scale effects that occur when output rises as a result of economic growth, even though that is typically driven by technological change. For but one example, the new technology of the transcontinental railway system turned much of the US economy from a subset of small markets, isolated from each other by high transport costs, into a single unified market whose size allowed the exploitation of scale effects that were inherent in the real world and could be shown in static models but were unavailable to small firms operating in regional markets.

1.2   Issues of Definition

The extensive literature on scale effects that we have surveyed for this Element contains many different and sometimes conflicting approaches. Scale effects are defined in three ways in the literature, two explicitly using a production or a cost function and one implicitly using a dynamic growth concept. Some authors sharply distinguish between the two explicitly defined concepts and argue that they are not wholly overlapping, while others switch back and forth between them without comment, appearing to hold that they are synonymous. Furthermore, there is little agreement among the various authors as to which of the two concepts applies in each of the cases studied. The third, the implicitly defined, growth-related concept, has been a source of confusion in the literature because it is given the same name as one of the explicitly defined concepts and, although both refer to different and complimentary phenomena, many authors have argued that one is right and the other, if not wrong, is both unimportant and misleading.

When a firm's unit costs change as its scale of operations changes, it is useful to distinguish between real and purely pecuniary scale effects. There is a real resource effect when there is a change in the amount of inputs per unit of output. There is a purely pecuniary effect when there is a change in the price of one or more of the firm's inputs with no related reduction in real resources used per unit of output.[1]

An example of a purely pecuniary effect is when the growth of an assembly firm allows it to gain market power over the many small suppliers of its parts. It can then transfer profits from the parts suppliers to itself with no change in real resource costs anywhere in the economy. An example of a real cause is when the increase in

---

[1] This distinction was once commonly made in the literature. However, of the many authors we surveyed, only the minority make the distinction between real and purely pecuniary effects. These are Bain (1968: 492), Bannock et al. (1984: 141–2), Becker (1999: 150), Bohm (2008: 189), Calhoun (2002: 357), Frank (2008: 359), Graaff (1987: 7599), Jackson (1996: 229) and Pearce (1992: 122). With the exceptions of Becker and Bain, these authors do not comment on the relative benefits or desirability of separating these two categories.

the assembler's size allows its parts suppliers to increase their size and reap more of their favourable scale effects. (Of course, to have unexploited scale effects in equilibrium, the suppliers must be price setters, not price takers, which is the normal case with differentiated products.) Note, however, that although this will appear as a real effect to the parts suppliers, it will appear, if the saving is passed on in terms of lower parts prices, as a pecuniary effect to the final goods producer. This example illustrates a general problem with the real–pecuniary distinction. Virtually all of the analysis of scale effects in the literature deals with a single firm. This would pose no problem if the production of raw materials, capital goods, other intermediate products and final goods were all integrated within a single firm. As it is, however, production is disintegrated into a large number of stages. As a result, what originates as a real cause upstream can appear as a pecuniary cause to downstream producers. We look at this issue in more detail at the beginning of Section 2.

Scale effects can be divided between those that arise at the level of individual items, usually capital equipment; the individual production facility, which with some violence to reality, we call a 'plant'; the whole firm; the industry; and the whole economy. This Element is mainly concerned with the first three sorts, all of which are internal to, i.e. under the control of, the firm. External effects at levels higher than the firm do exist, and we give some attention to them towards the end of the Element.

1.3   Approaches to Studying Scale Effects

The literature on scale effects typically considers a single firm that can be assumed to be producing some final consumers' good. In dealing with the scale effects facing this firm, three main approaches can be discerned. First, in microtheory texts, scale effects are treated almost exclusively in terms of the characteristics of a production function that relates physical inputs to physical output. The typical scale exercise is to alter all inputs by some constant multiple, λ, and observe the response of output, about which much more is said below. The analysis is usually purely formal and the underlying real-world causes of the characteristics of the production function that give rise to these effects are usually not considered in any detail, if at all. Then, if the firm's costs are required, given input prices allow a cost function to be derived from a production function.

Second, in the encyclopaedias, in most introductory textbooks and in some journal articles, the sources of scale effects are investigated in some detail. Our main concern in this Element is to follow in this tradition by seeking to explain, but in more depth than is usual in this literature, the reasons why a firm's costs vary in specific ways when its output varies over the long run with constant technological possibilities and in the very long run when these possibilities can change.

The third tradition is related to the growth literature and is considered in a later part of this section.

1.4   Displaying Scale Effects

Static scale effects, those that exist at some point in time, can be shown using either cost curves or production functions which lead to different but related definitions.

1.4.1   Through Cost Curves

The original graphic description of scale effects is due to Viner (1931) and is shown in Figure 1, a similar diagram to his. Input prices are assumed to be given and the curves then depend on the distinction between the long run, when all inputs can be varied, and the short run when some inputs are fixed, usually taken to be the plant and its equipment. The primitives in this treatment are the family of short-run average (or unit) total cost curves shown as the SRATC curves in the figure. Each curve relates to a different size of plant and possibly to a different production technique (as, for example, when mass production is used instead of craft-style production above some critical level of the firm's operations). The derived curve is the long-run average cost curve (LRAC curve), which is the envelope to the SRATC curves. If size of plant can only be varied discretely, the LRAC curve follows each SRATC

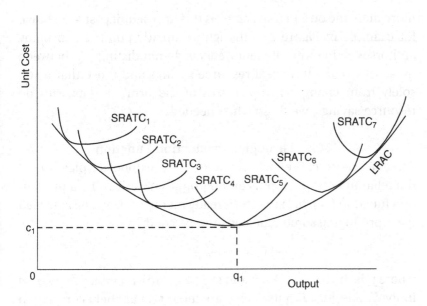

Figure 1 Short- and long-run costs

curve until it is intersected by the curve derived from a larger scale of operations. In the limit, if techniques can be varied continuously, each point the LRAC curve relates to a different size of plant.[2]

The typical textbook LRAC curve for a firm is U-shaped as shown in the figure. The negative-sloping section indicates what are typically called 'economies of scale' (EoS); the positively sloped section, 'diseconomies of scale' (DoS); and the horizontal portion, if one is assumed, the absence of scale economies (CoS).[3] We refer to these collectively as 'efficiency effects'. The output at the minimum point on this curve is called the minimum efficient scale or MES (q_1 in the figure); 'minimum' to allow for the fact that there may be

---

[2] Since it is costly to develop a production facility with a distinct SRATC curve, a firm will only be presented in practice with a finite number of possible plants and hence SRATC curves.

[3] It is worth noting that this modern usage is not quite that of Alfred Marshall's whose concept of internal economies 'is analytically looser than this [the modern usage], but richer in empirical content and, possibly, in philosophical insight' (Becattinni 2008: 419).

more than one output that achieves this lowest unit cost – as shown for example in Figure 2. Although as already pointed out, many authors who identify efficiency effects do not distinguish between those that result from real resource savings and those that result solely from changes in the prices of the firm's inputs with no resource savings, we do so when needed.

1.4.2   Through a Production Function

The analysis of scale effects in microtheory textbooks typically uses the relation between inputs and output as described by a production function for a firm that, as already mentioned, can be assumed to be producing some final consumers' good:

$$y_i = f(s_1, \ \ldots \ , s_n, \ s_{n+1}, \ \ldots \ , \ s_m) \tag{1.1}$$

where y_i is the ith final good and $s_1, \ldots, s_m$ are the service flows of m individual inputs. Inputs s_1 to s_n are those that are held constant in the short run while s_{n+1} to s_m are those that can be varied in both the short and long runs.

The returns effect is then defined as follows:

$$f(\lambda s_1, \ \ldots \ , \lambda s_m) = \alpha_\lambda f(s_1 \ldots \ , s_m), \tag{1.2}$$

where $\alpha_\lambda > \lambda$, $\alpha_\lambda = \lambda$ and $\alpha_\lambda < \lambda$ indicates respectively what are called increasing returns to scale (IRTS), constant returns to scale (CRTS) and decreasing returns to scale (DRTS).[4] We refer to these collectively as 'returns effects' and will have much more to say about them later in the Element. The previously introduced term 'scale effects' thus covers both returns and efficiency effects and any other changes due to alterations in the firm's scale of operations.

In the literature surveyed the large amount of disagreement on allocating sources between the returns and the efficiency categories suggests problems with the procedure of dividing all sources

---

[4] For example, '*Definition:* a technology exhibits increasing returns to scale if a proportionate increase in all inputs allows for a more than proportionate increase in outputs; in a single-output case, this implies a decreasing average cost curve' (Vassilakas 1987: 4625).

of scale effects into one or the other of these classes – problems that I discuss more fully in a subsequent section.

1.4.3   Through Growth

The above two ways of viewing scale effects are through static relations that exist at any point in time. A different view defines scale effects as something that can only be observed through changes rather than static relations. Authors in this tradition often quote Allyn Young (1928) as a precursor. Although he does not define the term 'increasing returns', taking its meaning as obvious, he has a conventional view of their sources, saying for example (p. 538): 'In so far as it is an adjustment to a new situation created by the growth of the market for the final products of industry the division of labour among industries is a vehicle of increasing returns.' His main concern is to argue that the exploitation of scale effects is permitted by the extension of the market for some industry. This may be due to economic growth or to a reallocation of resources into that market. Indeed, the figure in his concluding NOTE (p. 540) implicitly defines increasing returns as a falling opportunity cost of commodity X (e.g. manufactured goods) in terms of foregone Y (e.g. agricultural goods) as the production of X increases and that of Y decreases, which is resource reallocation not a growth phenomenon. So a discussion of Young really belongs in the later section on the conditions that lead to scale economies being exploited rather than as a novel concept of scale effects themselves.

But other authors who are in the Young tradition take a different view. Given that they are writing at much later dates, it is perhaps surprising that many in this tradition do not give a clear definition of what they mean by increasing returns, apparently, as with Young, taking its meaning as self-evident. But it is clear that they do not mean the definition of IRTS given above as they stress changes in both firms and products while rejecting any use of a production function with highly aggregated inputs. For example, Chandra and Sandilands write (2006: 201):

At the macro level, supply of inputs is not the main driving force in Young's conception of increasing returns; rather it is the size of the market, and the resulting greater specialisation at firm and industry levels. In this perspective, the concept of an aggregate production function suffers from a fallacy of composition: it does not depict the social picture, which may be much broader than the simple addition of its parts.

Although neither Young, nor Chandra and Sandilands (2006, 2009), nor Grieve in his reply to them find it necessary to give any clear definition of what they understand by increasing returns, Grieve (2010:128) does extract a clear definition of EoS from the Chandra and Sandilands paper. This is 'any cost reductions experienced as a firm, responding to increased demand for output, moves along a given, downward-sloping long run cost curve'. Although not unlike the standard definition that we use here, this one covers too much as EoS refers only to the slope of the long-run cost curve and not to where the firm is currently located on it, nor to why the firm might move from one point on it to another.

It would appear from the above, and other related, statements that Chandra and Sandilands, and others in the same tradition, see EoS as a static concept involving a given long-run cost curve and increasing returns as a dynamic concept involving shifts in that curve, shifts that are associated with economic growth in general and increases in the size of the market in particular. We should also note that one of the causes of the many confusions in the discussions of scale effects in the literature is the failure of economists studying evolutionary behaviour of growing economies to distinguish their concept of returns from the static concept found in the majority of the modern literature on scale effects.[5]

---

[5] Chandra and Sandilands (2006: 200–202)make a big point about EoS not being important for increasing returns as they understand the concept. This is fair enough since for them one is a static concept and the other is a dynamic one. But IRTS as defined both here, and in the literature on scale effects that we have surveyed, is closely related to EoS because with input prices constant, the existence of the former implies the existence of the latter.

Although the reciprocal relation between growth and the exploitation of scale effects is clear (see Section 5), it is not clear that any new, largely implicit, dynamic definition of increasing returns is needed to study it. The standard theory of the sources of scale effects as covered in this Element seems to provide sufficient tools for studying the scale effects of growth in markets that result from growth in either part or all of the economy.

In this context Setterfield (2001: 489) is the only author in our survey who overlaps with this dynamic approach by distinguishing between what he terms static and dynamic scale effects. He defines static IRTS as increasing returns from an increase in the scale of production at a point in time, and dynamic IRTS as the technological and/or organisational transformation of the production process over time as the scale of production increases. Setterfield's examples of static IRTS are spatial relationships such as that between surface area and volume, while his examples of what he calls dynamic IRTS include capital and labour specialisation and process indivisibilities in the context of demand-driven expansion. But each of these latter effects can be studied in a static context. Both can be defined at a point in time as alternative locations on a long-run cost curve, while to move from one such point to another clearly takes place over time and will require some incentive such as an expanded market. So once again a new dynamic definition of scale effects does not seem to be required.

1.4.4 Replication and Reconfiguration

The plant with all of its capital equipment is the main input held constant in the short run and thus one of the main locations of scale effects over the long run. If a firm's scale of operations is to be increased, the capital goods that deliver the needed capital services must be altered. The firm is then choosing from new sets of capital goods, all of which embody known technological knowledge. Two types of choices are possible. Either the firm's capital may be *replicated*, which means creating more units identical to those already in use, or it may be *reconfigured*, which means using differently designed capital goods. For example, when an airline buys more units of a 150-seat aircraft already in their fleet, this is replication; when it replaces its fleet of 150-seat aircraft with an off-the-shelf purchase of 300-seat aircraft, this is reconfiguration.

If an airline reconfigures its aircraft and related capital goods in the long run in order to increase the scale of its output, the new capital may be more efficient than the original at delivering its service input to the firm for two distinct reasons.

First, consider the production of the aircraft. Typically with today's technology, the 300-seat aircraft will have lower costs per passenger-kilometre than the 150-seat aircraft. The reasons for this are investigated at length later in the Element under the heading 'Efficiencies of Design' (Section 1.5). It should be obvious, however, that we cannot describe the differences in the production of the two aircraft as being simple multiples of the physical inputs used in the aircraft manufacturer's given production function. Each aircraft will have its own distinct production process that uses some different and some identical physical inputs the latter in altered proportions.

Second, consider the airline that goes over from a 150- to 300-seat aircraft. Major structural readjustments in its production process may not be needed, although even in this simple case, all of the firm's inputs will not have to be increased in proportion. The same computer-driven reservation system and the same-sized cockpit crew may do the job, and, while the cabin crew will have to be increased, their number will typically not need to be doubled. Moreover, the economies inherit in larger aircraft will mean that the fuel used will rise by less than in proportion to the number of passengers carried, and so on.

More generally, when the firm increases its scale of operations, increasing its output of the number of passenger miles carried, we cannot assume that the types of capital goods and labour whose services it uses will be nothing more than variations in the quantities in an unchanged set of generic inputs to its production function. Instead as scale increases, more specialisation of both labour and capital goods may occur, requiring different types of labour, capital goods and intermediate inputs of the nuts-and-bolts variety. Often new jobs and new types of capital will be needed for activities that were not required at a lower and less specialised production process.

In summary, the firm is adopting a new production process requiring some new inputs, some different amounts of the existing inputs and possibly a wholly new organisation of its production processes.

So, each point on the firm's LRAC curve is defined by a different relation between inputs and output with at least some different inputs of various types of the services of both capital and variable factors and in which those inputs that are used in more than one of these production processes often have different marginal products in each.

1.4.5 Two Types of Production Functions

The above discussion raises an important question: How are we to describe the relation between inputs and output in long-run situations when techniques of production typically vary greatly from one scale of operation to another? To deal with this question we distinguish two different definitions of the production function (hereafter PF).

Two PF Definitions

Definition 1: The type-1 PF gives the maximum output that can be produced by each given bundle of inputs *on the assumption that the firm is using a specific technology of production.*

In this case, the inputs can be defined in terms of actual physical quantities, as they almost always are in the literature. Of course, some level of aggregation is necessary to prevent the PF having thousands of inputs, but they can be physical units such as hours worked by various types of labour, units of energy, raw materials, semi-finished goods and the services of various types of machines and structures. It follows that no single, type-1 PF can apply to different long runs where different production techniques require different physical inputs used in different ways and in different proportions. Instead, as the scale of output rises progressively, there will be a series of type-1 PFs that are consistent with Viner's original analysis. Although he dealt exclusively with cost curves and not with PFs, each of his short-run cost curves refers to a plant of a different scale.[6] As discussed

---

[6] Viner (1931: 205–6) lists three reasons why costs may vary over the long run: operating a given plant with a different intensity of use, changes in the scale of

earlier, the primitives here are the short-run curves, each one referring to a different plant often using different equipment, types of labour and intermediate inputs. Although he does not use the term, this implies that the short-run cost curves are derived from a series of plants each having a different PF. The envelope long-run cost curve is derived by the exercise of finding the most efficient short-run curve to adopt for each given output in the long run.

Definition 2: The type-2 PF gives the maximum output that can be produced by each given bundle of inputs *on the assumption that the firm can utilise any technology of production that is currently available.*

As argued above, when the firm changes the scale of its output in the long run, it is altering its 'plant', which often means employing different technologies of production such as machines that have different capacities and do different jobs, for example, moving from a craft-style to a mass-production-style production process. From the point of view of the Viner approach, Definition 2 gives a meta-PF that covers all these different production techniques in one function. Now the LRAC curve is not derived from the short-run curves. Instead, given input prices, it can be derived directly from the PF.

Some of the theorists whom we have studied explicitly make the point that different production processes are used at different scales of production.[7] Others do so implicitly without saying it in so many words.[8] Yet others just relate the LRAC curve to a single PF

---

plant and replication of identical plants. It is not clear how the first reason differs from the short run situation of varying intensity of use of a fixed amount of capital, while the third is to be considered later in this Element. This leaves the second, using different plants having different scales of operation.

[7] Baumol (1977: 290), Blaug (1978: 397), DeSerpa (1985: 207), Eaton et al. (2012: 185–6), Kamerschen and Valentine (1977: 232–3), Mansfield (1979: 182), Shone (1981: 158) and Sher and Pinola (1986: 96) all say that at different scales of output the firm will use different production techniques. Mahanty (1980: 229) does say that each different short run curve is derived from a different production function, but he derives each of these from a single type-2 PF using a different amount of an input that is fixed in the short run and using the same variable inputs each time.

[8] Nicholson (1979: 188) and Quirk (1987: 181) seem to imply this without stating it explicitly

and do not say explicitly what changes are occurring between different points on that curve.[9] In all cases, however, the authors use a single PF to describe the firm's long-term behaviour. Varian alone among all of those we have studied seems to recognise that when different techniques are used, his one-production-function analysis cannot be applied. He writes that when subdividing inputs (1992: 15, italics added): '[T]here may be some minimal scale of operation so that producing output below this scale involves different techniques. Once the minimal scale of operation is reached, *larger levels* of output can be produced by replication.' He does not analyse what happens below this minimal scale that is reached by decreasing the number of possible replicated plants until only one remains. But this is where the LRAC curve takes on a negative slope because scale effects operate when different techniques are embodied in plants with different optimal scales of output.

Morroni (1992: especially 1–3 and 9–11) gives a discussion, with many references, of why a single production function is a poor tool for analysing firm behaviour when its scale of operations is altered. While accepting much of the force of his argument, I follow here the main line of the literature in treating scale effects within the confines of production function analysis, either PF-1 or PF-2. I do this for two reasons. First, in order to critique the treatment of scale effects in the literature, I must follow all those writers who express them in terms of the characteristics of a production function. Second, I believe that what matters for this Element, but not necessarily for other lines of investigation related to economic growth, can be studied using production functions.

Variables in the PF

All writers who are explicit about the variables in the PF state that these are actual physical quantities. Since this is an important point, we illustrate with a few examples of what writers say when

---

[9] Binger and Hoffman (1988: 258–60), Griffiths and Wall (2000: 163–73), Hirshleifer et al. (2005: 177) and Miller (1978: 200) say nothing about what techniques are being used at different scales of production.

they are explicit about specific inputs in the PF (italics added to all quotations): '*The level of skill of workers (as compared with their pay), the quality and price of the materials used, the type of machine, and the ability of management*' (Ammer and Ammer 1984: 368-9); '*labour, capital, raw materials, etc.*' (Bannock et al. 2003: 311); '*The output might be kilowatt hours of electricity per year; [input 1] might be tons of coal per year; and [input 2] might be maintenance hours per year*' (Smith 1968: 512); '*A mining firm, in order to extract ore, has to employ land . . . together with labor, buildings, electric power, gasoline, and machines. The technological relation between such inputs and firm's output is called the production function*' (Hirshleifer et al. 2005: 340). More generally, Varian (1992: 4) Kamerschen and Valentine (1977: 184) and Jehle and Reny (2001: 127) define the PF as an array of physical inputs and a single output and then leave it at that, while Binger and Hoffman (1988: 231, 258), DeSerpa (1985: 168), Mahanty (1980: 146, 164) and Nicholson (1979: 131-2) define it as including specific quantities but then use the aggregated capital labour, K-L, formulation for their detailed analysis. Slightly differently, Shone (1981: 105-8) uses the general quantity form until he gets to the scale discussion where he switches without explanation to the K-L formulation. Finally, Griffiths and Wall (2000: 151), Quirk (1987: 144) and Sher and Pinola (1986: 5) all use the K-L formulation from the outset.[10]

There are three serious problems with this common view that the variables in the PF are real physical inputs. The first relates to the assumption of the substitutability of inputs in most production function analysis. Many, in some cases most, inputs at this micro

---

[10] All authors are clear that the production function relates physical inputs to physical output so when they use two aggregate inputs such as capital and labour, this must be assumed to be for illustration only and that a solution exists to the old capital controversy as to what is meant by different *quantities* of capital when they are bundles of very different physical entities. The only author to make explicit reference to this problem in the present context is Mansfield who writes (1979: 145), 'Another important problem is the measure-ment of capital input. The principle difficulty stems from the fact that the stock of capital is composed of various types and ages of machines, buildings and inventory. Combining them into a single measure . . . is a formidable problem.'

level are complementary to each other and need to be used in approximately fixed proportions. Thus, although it is possible to think of substituting between labour and capital defined at a high level of aggregation, it makes little sense to consider substitution between such specific physical inputs as needles and thread. Morroni, who discusses this issue of complementarity among inputs in some detail, observes: 'It is hard to conceive of a form of textile production in which yarn could be replaced by machine-hours or man-hours' (1992: 29). Probably for this reason, most who use production functions for specific analytical studies work at high levels of aggregation, such as labour, capital and materials, where substitution among these inputs can be considered as a common case. But this is not what they say they are going to do when they define the inputs as specific physical entities as noted above.

The second problem is that, as already observed, the variables in use alter in myriad ways from one scale of operation to another. For example, the vast majority of the tools used in a labour-intensive, craft form of production are different from those used in Fordist mass-production factory, which in turn differ from those used in a modern roboticised factory. So are the needles and finger guards used in a textile factory using foot-operated sewing machines different from their counterparts used in a mechanised form of production of the same product. If we are to avoid the PF having a vast number of inputs, most of which are unused at most scales of production, we must again define the inputs as quantity-index numbers for broad categories, such as capital (K), labour (L) and, when needed, materials (M) – the latter can be important as many modern technologies are much less resource using per unit of output at large scales than at lower scales of activity. The weighting of individual items in each such index must use their prices. Although at this level of aggregation we have macro not microeconomics, it is possible to divide labour into subgroups, such as skilled, semi-skilled and unskilled, and subdivide capital in various ways. However, the definition of each input must not be such as to include the specific physical items listed by the writers mentioned in the previous paragraph; they must instead be flexible enough to include these items in broad generic groups.

The third and more serious problem related to the inputs in the PF being real physical units concerns the measurement of scale effects. The problem arises only with the type-2 PF, which covers various scales of output in one function. As noted above, returns to scale are typically measured by multiplying all inputs by some constant λ and seeing if the output changes by a multiple that is more than, less than or the same as λ. But this operation makes no sense when there is a detailed list of the physical inputs used at any one scale of operations since, as already noted, when the scale of output changes significantly, firms typically adopt new production techniques that often use new tools, new kinds of labour and new produced inputs. So once again we see the need to use broad quantity indexes such as total labour and total capital.

But even this aggregate usage does not avoid all of the difficulties associated with the definition of returns effects. Even in the simplest two-input case that uses indexes of capital and labour, the most efficient capital/labour ratio typically changes as the scale of output changes with input prices constant. Thus, the equi-proportionate multiple experiments can be misleading. Doubling the set of specific physical inputs that many writers refer to is in most cases a nonsense operation that no engineer would contemplate. Doubling both of the generic inputs, L and K, that are used at any scale of output may cause output to less than double (if a larger plant is created using these input ratios) or just double (if exiting plant is replicated), while *varying the input ratios at a doubled total cost* may arrive at an optimum for that cost that more than doubles output – as, for example, when the firm moves from craft to mass-production techniques.

This critique of the returns to scale definition reveals what should be obvious: we cannot tell if the firm will encounter favourable scale effects from knowledge of the PF alone. We need prices of the inputs that allow us to maximise by calculating the combination of inputs that either minimises total cost for any given output or maximises output for any given total cost. There is one exception: if all expansion paths for any given set of relative input prices are linear through the origin, the optimum proportions in which to combine the inputs do not vary with the scale of output. In this case the returns definition will correctly identify the existence of IRTS, CRTS and DRTS. Here, however, we have something that has little empirical relevance in a world of ubiquitous non-constant scale effects related to capital goods with differentiated parts. In all such cases, the optimum ratio in which to use the aggregate inputs will vary with the scale of output and the returns definition will not necessarily identify the existence of favourable or unfavourable scale effects arising from the nature of the PF.

Returns and Efficiency Effect's in the PF

If everything that confers costs on the firm is included as inputs in the PF, and if the prices of these inputs are given, we do not have two independent sources of scale effects, one arising from the PF and one from the cost function. To determine scale effects from the PF, we need to know the input prices so as to determine the least-cost way of producing any given output, and when this is done for all scales of output, we have the cost function.[11] But this relation

---

[11] In certain circumstances the duality theorem allows one to 'recover' a production function from a given cost function. This is not the place to go into the details of this procedure but suffice it to say (1) that input prices need to be constant, which, as we will soon see, is not necessarily the case when the scale effects are located upstream in capital goods producing firms and (2) that problems arise if firms are price setters, rather than price takers, as are all firms selling differentiated goods and services. On the latter issue, Jorgenson (2008: 671) states: 'Under increasing returns and competitive markets for output and all inputs, producer equilibrium is not defined by profit maximization, since no maximum of profit exists [under perfectly competitive conditions]. However, in regulated industries the price of output is set by regulatory authority. Given demand for output as a function of the regulated price, the level of output is exogenous to the producing unit.' He conducts his subsequent duality analysis under IRTS with this assumption. Alternatively it can be assumed that firms all charge the same constant markup over all units of production and all time periods, and then do the calculation for every firm independent of any aggregation – also very restrictive conditions. Neither of these special situations covers the cases that are of prime interest here: price setting monopolists, oligopolists or monopolistic competitors that face EoS that cannot be fully exploited because of their current equilibrium positions.

depends on (1) all things that affect a firm's costs at all scales of output being included in its PF and (2) input prices being constant. If things such as selling costs are not included in the PF, a firm may increase its output by the proportion λ and encounter CRTS but EoS if input quantities increase by λ while selling costs increase by less. Also, if an increase in a firm's size increases its market power over its input suppliers, its input prices can fall, creating an EoS with no change in the relation been physical inputs and output. More importantly, as we observed above and will illustrate more fully under the subheading 'Scale Effects in Two-Stage Production' at the beginning of Section 2, real scale effects achieved by a capital goods producer may be transmitted to the final goods producer in the form of pecuniary effects.

As we will see later in this Element, when authors discuss the sources of favourable scale effects, such as more efficient capital or greater division of labour, they disagree in almost all cases as to whether the source causes an IRTS or an EoS. This should not surprise us in the light of our arguments both that the standard definition of returns to scale is deficient and that production actually takes place in multiple stages.

Indeed, it is not obvious that there is any gain in distinguishing between these two concepts. However, if we wish to do so, the following definitions may suffice: *returns to scale* occur when there is a change in a firm's unit cost of production that would have occurred if all input prices had remained constant, while *economies or diseconomies of scale* occur if there are changes in a firm's unit cost including those that would not have occurred if input prices had remained constant. Thus, returns to scale are located in the relation between a firm's inputs and its output and these give rise to economies of scale which can also arise from sources such as input price changes due to changes in market power or upstream scale effects.

For the rest of this study we use the type-1 definition where each different technique of production has its own PF, each one of which may differ from the others in the nature of inputs and the marginal rates of substitution among them at various scales of output. Those who wish to continue with the type-2 PF definition can think of returns to scale when we speak of efficiencies of design as defined below.

Further Problems with the PF

We note in passing that there are other serious problems connected with both of the definitions of a PF. To see these, consider the concept of technical efficiency, an engineering concept. Let there be a single product produced by a bundle of inputs: (1) A *bundle of inputs* is being used with technical efficiency if you could not use that bundle to produce more of that product than it is currently producing; (2) a *good* is being produced with technical efficiency if there is no other way to produce it using less of all inputs that are now being used. Condition (1) looks at the efficiency with which a specific bundle of inputs is being used while condition (2) looks at the efficiency with which a given output is being produced.[12]

Most definitions of the PF consider only condition (1), for example: 'The production function for a firm shows the maximum output that can be produced with specific levels of inputs, given the available technology' (McAuliffe 1999: 165). Such definitions implicitly assume that there is no problem with condition (2). That is they assume that when we define the maximum output that can be produced with each possible input combination, there is no possibility that any of these will be technically inefficient in the sense that the indicated output could be produced with fewer of all inputs. If we accept that such inefficiency is possible, and knowledge of real technologies shows that this is a possibility in many cases, then some of the points in input space may not be efficient points and hence not part of the PF because, although they fulfil condition (1), they violate condition (2). Or to put it another way, the PF will not span the whole of the input space. This issue is elaborated in the Appendix B under the heading 'Alternative Factor

---

[12] These concepts do not require prices. In contrast economic efficiency, which does not concern us at this point, looks at costs and defines output to be efficiently produced if there is no other input combination that would produce that output at a lower cost.

Combinations at a Given Output'. But since these complications do not affect our subsequent analysis (but do raise serious issues concerning the treatment of the PF in theory textbooks) discussion of them is confined to the appendix.

1.5 Efficiencies of Design

For the reasons outlined earlier, there will typically be scale effects associated with the firm's change of scale because different capital goods and different production process will be used at different scales of output. In our approach this means that one type-1 PF is substituted for another type-1 PF.

We now define a new concept called 'efficiencies of design' and refer to EoD, DoD and CoD when the replacement of an original production process by a new one described by a new type-1 PF leads to a fall, a rise or no change in the unit cost of output – for example, a fall when we move from any of the PFs that give rise to the SRATC curves labelled 1 to 4 in Figure 1 to a curve that is one number higher. Efficiencies of design are similar to efficiencies of scale except that they explicitly refer to movements from one PF-1 to another caused by a reconfiguration of the capital goods being used or the organisation of production, whereas EoS (1) do not specify what type of production function lies behind the observed cost changes and (2) may refer to changes in costs not due to design changes such as changes in input prices as result of changes in market power.

The sources of each of these implied variations in efficiency are the subject of subsequent sections. Note, however, that there is one major exception to the need to refer to the design effect, which is when the firm increases its scale of operations by replicating existing plants. No new design is involved; it is a case of just more of the same. In all other cases, however, there will typically be design effects when one PF is substituted for another. If one wishes, one can say that the resulting changes in unit costs are the result of returns to scale in a type-2 PF. But this is merely a description, not an explanation. We still need to ask why the type-2 PF has the shape that it does, and that takes us to explanations based on what we call efficiencies of design, which we consider at length in Section 2.

1.6 Scale Effects and Firm Size

Some further ground clearing is needed because in subsequent treatments we need to consider firms in equilibrium on all sections of their LRAC curves, those with negative, positive and zero slopes. Although there are many things that influence the size of firms, what we need to consider here is the relation between scale effects and size (as well as some related matters). Indeed, two of the most important applications of knowledge about scale effects is (i) to contribute to explaining the size of firms in particular industries and (ii) to identify natural, scale-induced barriers to entry – an absence of which helps to explain the prevalence of man-made barriers to entry in many industries.[13]

1.6.1 Implications of MES Relative to Market Size

As is well known, if a firm's MES is at a very large output relative to the market demand at the corresponding market price, there will be room for only one firm producing at or near its minimum efficient scale – a natural monopoly. If it occurs at not quite so large an output, there may be room for more than one firm. In situations of duopoly or oligopoly there is nothing in competitive forces to prevent the competing firms from being in equilibrium on the negative-sloping sections of their LRAC curves. If the MES is at a very small output, there will be room for many firms and there

---

[13] Long ago Jo Bain, one of the pioneers of Industrial Organisation, measured scale economies in a large sample of firms by estimating the proportion of the market supplied by a single plant operating at its MES and the rise in unit cost at an output equal to half that at its MES. Industries with 'very important' scale economies at that time were automobiles and typewriters and those with 'moderately important' ones were cement, farm machines, rayon, steel and tractors. He found that product differentiation was a major barrier to entry whose source is complex, and includes heavy advertising (Bain 1956: 142–3). Interestingly, three of the industries with the highest man-made barriers were among those with the lowest natural scale barriers to entry.

may exist something approaching a situation in which each firm regards itself as a price taker rather than a price setter, assuming that they sell an undifferentiated product.

Although empirical observations support these generalisations (see, for example, Chandler 1990), they might seem at odds with Young's insistence (1928: 527) that there is a 'common error of assuming that wherever increasing returns operate there is necessarily an effective tendency towards monopoly'. Someone who assumes that scale effects are sufficient for the emergence of monopoly is clearly wrong. But much evidence shows that large-scale effects are often associated with industries containing a small number of firms, occasionally one monopolist but more frequently a few oligopolists.[14]

Eatwell (2008: 140) takes issue with the use of scale effects as an explanation of the size of firms when he writes:

> Marshall himself recognized the incompatibility of the assumption of competition and presence of increasing returns ... Piero Sraffa ... exposed the entire exercise as ill-founded by demonstrating that neither increasing nor decreasing returns to scale are compatible with the assumption of perfect competition in the theory of the firm or of the partial-equilibrium industry supply curve – a result which, although prominently published and debated, has apparently escaped the notice of those who still draw that bogus U-shaped cost curve whilst purporting to analyse the equilibrium of the competitive firm.

Of course, there is nothing incompatible with perfect competition for firms to have a U-shaped LRATC curves; what is incompatible is for a firm's current production to be either in the range of *unexploited* internal EoS or in the range where it is encountering DoS. In other words, as textbooks correctly, not ignorantly, point out, every profit-maximising firm that is a price

---

[14] Nothing said here contradicts Schumpeter's point that the resulting high profits will encourage other firms to find ways to make innovations that provide end runs around the position(s) of the established firm(s), for example, by inventing close substitutes that will erode the profits of incumbents.

taker in a free market must be producing at the minimum point on its LRAC, whether U-shaped of otherwise (a point that is usually assumed to be unique for analytical convenience, even if not always for descriptive realism). However, as long as a firm is a price setter, not a price taker (as, for example, is any firm selling a differentiated product) there is nothing inconsistent with its operating on the negatively sloped portion of its LRAC curve – i.e. having unexploited internal economies of scale. Chamberlin's tangency solution is but one example, while price setting oligopolists in industries with either natural or man-made barriers to entry, provide many others. In what follows, we assume that firms can be in equilibrium with such unexploited scale economies.

1.6.2   Replication with Variable Unit Costs

Once the MES of a single plant has been reached and where replication of plants is possible, a firm's unit costs are usually assumed to be constant.[15] But this is so only for integer multiples of the MES of that plant. Now consider desired outputs that are non-integer multiples of q_1 as illustrated in Figure 2. Although it is hard to avoid language that sounds as if a movement over time is being considered, the analysis is of alternates for a single choice of plants to produce a given output. To produce any output greater than q_1 and less than $2q_1$ the firm has two choices. It can use one plant whose associated unit cost exceeds c_1 or it can use two plants, one producing at its MES of q_1 and the other smaller plant producing the extra desired amount in excess of q_1. We refer to these respectively as the large-plant and the two-plant solutions. For small increases in output above q_1 the large-plant solution will be the superior choice. For example, to build the minimum sized plant that would produce 1 unit when the desired output is q_1+1 and underutilize it would result in a very high unit cost of that output. In contrast, for a

---

[15] For example, Frevert (1997: 1374): 'Since any physical production process can be duplicated, all production should adhere to constant returns to scale.'

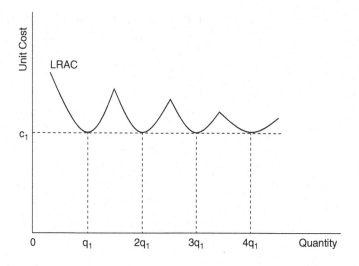

Figure 2 Variable scale effect with replication

large increase above q_1 the two-plant solution will be the superior choice. For example, if the desired output is $2q_1-1$, the unit cost of the second plant will be only slightly above c_1 while the unit cost of the larger plant will be well above that figure.

One might think that the changeover from the large-plant to the two-plant solution would be when the unit cost of the large plant equaled the unit cost of the smaller plant under the two-plant solution. But this must occur at a lesser output because with the larger plant the cost of all units of output are above c_1 while with the two-plant solution only the units produced by the smaller of the two plants will incur a cost of over c_1. To determine the change-over output let the total cost of output in the one-plant solution be $(q_1+\Delta q)(c_1+\Delta c)$ and for the two plant solution be $c_1q_1 +c_s\Delta q$, where c_s is the unit cost of production in the small plant. Equating these and solving for c_s gives:

$$c_s = [\Delta c(q_1 + \Delta q) + \Delta q c_1)]/\Delta q$$

For example, let the MES occur at 100 units of output with a unit cost of 10 and the larger desired output be 110 with a unit cost of 11 when produced by a single plant. The two-plant solution will then be the superior choice if the unit cost associated with the smaller plant is less than 21.

Assuming that the large-plant solution is the superior choice for some range of output starting at q_1, the LRAC curve takes the shape shown in Figure 2 between q_1 and $2q_1$. The kink occurs at the changeover where the rising cost associated with the large-plant solution is replaced by the falling cost associated with the two-plant solution. More generally, if we consider non-integer production between nq_1 and $(n+1)q_1$, the choice between the two solutions is the same at the margin for any n, with (i) the two-plant solution applying to the nth plant producing at q_1 units and a smaller plant and (ii) the large-plant solution with one plant producing an output between nq_1 and $(n+1)q_1$. But since the firm's total output produced by all the plants operating at their MESs is larger the larger is n, the average cost in the interval between nq_1 and $(n+1)q_1$ is lower the larger is n. Hence the kinked LRAC curve between the each of the multiples of q_1 gets flatter and flatter as n increases, until in the limit it approaches a straight line joining the two extreme MES points.

If output of the plant that produces q_1 at its MES is large relative to the market demand at the corresponding price, the range over which the firm will build a plant that has a higher unit cost than c_1 can also be large. This challenges the *a priori* argument found so often in the literature that firms will never encounter increasing costs if replication is possible. Here there are no hidden inputs and although replication is possible, it is not efficient over some ranges of output.

Almost all of the surveyed authors mention replication as a sources of CoS and/or CRTS. Varian is among the few authors in our survey who directly deal with the fact that the replication argument for constant return to scale applies only to integer multiples of the output at the MES of the most efficient size of plant. He writes (1992: 15): 'Another circumstance where constant returns to scale may be violated is when we want to scale operation up by non-integer amounts ... how do we do one and half times what we were doing before?' He does not answer this question except to observe that 'such cases are only important when the scale of production is small relative to the minimum scale of output'. This will not be the case for the price taking firms that are the usual case in the micro textbooks, but it is the common case in manufacturing and many service industries where firms are price setters and the number of firms in the industry is small.

1.6.3   Replication with Non-Plant-Specific Fixed Costs

Another interesting case arises with costs that are specific to the firm but do not vary with either the firm's total output or its number of plants. The literature often mentions management functions that may not need to be increased in proportion to the increases in output when new plants are added (Griffiths & Wall 2000: 172; McConnell et al. 2012: 154). But these are usually sources of relatively small savings. We deal with cases where this effect is large in Section 3. So all we need to observe here is that such costs confer a falling average total cost even when the output is varied by replicating existing plants. So, if in the absence of such costs the firm would encounter constant average cost for outputs that are integer multiples of the optimum-size plant, increasing output by increasing the number of plants causes average total cost to be declining. So the firm's size is not limited by technical factors but will instead be limited by total demand if it is a monopolist, or competition with other similar firms if it has competitors.

2   The Sources of Positive Scale Effects

We now consider the major sources of positive scale effects, both those that have been alleged in the literature and those that our analysis suggests to be important. We also discuss a few other minor sources in order to consider all of the sources listed by at least one of the many authors that we have surveyed.

2.1 Scale Effects in Two-Stage Production

Scale effects, both favourable and unfavourable, are typically divided in the literature between those that are internal and those that are external to the firm. Since all but one of the works cited in this Element study a single firm that can be assumed to be a producer of some final good, scale effects that are external to that firm but internal to a firm producing the capital goods that it uses are typically classified as being internal to the final goods producer. Only one work on our survey considered scale effects in a model that exploits the fact, fundamental to early capital theorists, that capitalist production is two-stage production with a capital good being made in stage one and then used to assist in producing some final good in the second stage. We elaborate on the two-stage analysis of Lipsey, Carlaw and Bekar (2005: 393) which, although it contains an important flaw, does illustrate some key points about scale effects in a two-stage production process.

Let there be a firm that is in the business of pasturing other people's horses. One square unit of fenced space, the capital good, is required for the accommodation of one horse, the final service output being one horse pastured. The grass is free and the only production cost of final output is the service of the fenced pasture, which is continuously variable in its production. When the firm wishes to provide pasture for more horses, it orders an increase in the size of its fenced field.

The final output of horses pastured depends on the area of the pasture in a linear homogeneous function where one square unit of pasture, P, is sufficient to maintain one horse, H.

$$H = P \tag{II.1}$$

The typical treatment found in the literature models only the PF for final goods as in (II.1) above and in this case there are no apparent scale effects.

Now consider the PF for the capital good, P, which is created by enclosing land by F feet of fence according to the following PF:

$$P = (F/4)^2 \qquad (\text{II.2})$$

Here we see scale effects:

$$dP/dF = F/2 \qquad (\text{II.3})$$

which is increasing in F. To check, multiply F in equation (II.2) by λ to get:

$$P = (\lambda F/4)^2 = \lambda^2 (F/4)^2. \qquad (\text{II.4})$$

Assume that the fence is built in period 1 and lasts z years after construction, covering periods 2 to $z+1$, and costs \$1 per foot to build with no maintenance costs until it expires. (Thus the returns and economies concepts can be treated interchangeably in the capital goods industry.) Assume that pasture is rented out for equal yearly payments over that period. The supplying firm wishes to make a return of $r\%$ on its investment. So it must charge a price, y per unit of pasture, such that the discounted present value of the stream of payments equals the production cost plus a desired return on the investment in the fence, $F(1 + r)$. Assuming the desired rate of profit is the same as the discount rate, the price that must be charged per unit of pasture is:

$$\frac{(1+r)F}{(F/4)^2} = \sum_{t=2}^{z+1} \frac{y}{(1+r)^t} \qquad (\text{II.5})$$

or

$$\frac{16(1+r)}{F} = y \sum_{t=2}^{z+1} \frac{1}{(1+r)^t} \qquad (\text{II.6})$$

Letting the constant summation term be C, we have

$$y = \frac{16(1+r)}{CF} \qquad (\text{II.7})$$

which is decreasing in F. So, the price charged per unit of pasture falls as pasture size, and hence the number of horses pastured, is increased. Note that the capital goods industry has IRTS while the final goods industry has CRTS. The two taken together produce EoS for the final goods producer.

Although a special case, this example has some general implications. Scale effects can occur even when the relevant PF for the final good displays constant returns to scale. In the present case, there is an IRTS from the point view of the capital goods industry, while from the point of view of the final goods producer these real changes become an EoS in the form of a reduction in the cost of its capital service input. Thus one must look to the first stage, capital goods industry, in a two-stage production process to understand the scale effects that have their source in the nature of capital goods. From the economy's point of view there is a real resource-saving scale economy, although it shows up as a reduction in the cost of an input to the final goods producer. It is difficult (impossible?) to compress this behaviour into a single PF for the final goods producer who encounters constant returns in terms of its own physical inputs. (Indeed Lipsey, Carlaw and Bekar (2005) tried to do this but erred by substituting the PF for the capital good into the PF for the final good, thereby implicitly assuming that the capital good must be replaced each period.) The difficulties in studying two-stage scale effect in a treatment that uses only one PF possibly accounts for the large amount of disagreement that we chronicle below in designating sources of scale effects as causing either returns or efficiency effects.

2.2   Pervasiveness of Scale Effects

A general proof of the pervasiveness of scale effects with respect to all types of capital goods was provided some time ago by Eaton and Lipsey (1977). Here is an intuitive statement of their formal argument.

Definition: The amount of services embodied in a capital good is a measure of its 'lumpiness'. Since the amount of embodied services varies directly with durability, *endogenous lumpiness* is created when capital goods are produced to be more durable than is absolutely necessary for them to do some specific job.

Assumptions: (1) The interest rate is positive. (2) A decision must be made on the amount of durability to build into any capital good, whether the minimum necessary or some larger amount. (3) The technology of building capital goods displays constant CoS effects in the sense that the reconfiguration of a capital good to alter its durability so that it embodies λ more or less capital services implies that the cost of producing that capital good changes in the same proportion, λ.

Implication: Interest costs are minimised by minimising the capital good's durability.

Empirical observation: It is a matter of simple observation that virtually all capital goods are made more durable than they could be, a phenomenon that Eaton and Lipsey call endogenous temporal lumpiness or indivisibility.

Contradiction: The empirical observation of endogenous lumpiness is inconsistent with the implication drawn from the three basic assumptions: unit cost of delivering a capital good's services is minimised by minimising durability.

Conclusion: Since assumption (1) is known to be true and assumption (2) may be taken to be to verified by observation of the great majority of capital goods (we know of no exceptions), the conclusion is that assumption (3) must be false. This assumption is then altered as follows: *There is a universal scale effect in embodying services in capital goods: as durability of the capital good is increased, there is some range, starting from the minimum necessary for the good to do it job, over which the services that it embodies rise faster than the cost of adding to the good's durability.*

The ubiquity of scale effects related to capital goods is shown by this proof based on the existence of endogenously determined lumpiness or durability. More durability usually implies more strength, different handling characteristics, more ability to deal with random shocks and many other sources of scale effects related to both statistical and natural laws that are considered in a later section. The one place in which the present treatment is in disagreement with the Eaton-Lipsey paper is in their treatment of lumpiness and indivisibility as identical. We return to this issue below where we discuss the various meanings that are given in the literature to the concept of indivisibility.

2.3 Scale Effects due to Indivisibilities

The concept of indivisibilities plays a large role in the literature of scale effects. To make the concept more precise we outline several distinct but related types of divisibility and indivisibility. As we will show later, each one of these has been used by one or more of our authors to explain scale effects, although we argue that most of these do not do so. Furthermore, some authors cite more than one type, and by treating them all as the same indivisibility, they cause confusion. We confine ourselves to capital goods, such as individual machines and whole plants, although much of what we say applies equally to other types of goods, such as consumers' durables.

We distinguish two basic meanings of indivisibility, *ex post* and *ex ante*, and some variations of each version.

2.3.1   Ex post Divisibility and Indivisibility

This refers to altering an individual capital good or plant once it has been produced. A good or plant is *ex post* divisible if, once produced, it can be subdivided such that its parts can do the same type of job as can be done by the whole. For example, a one-ton bag of wheat, once produced, can be subdivided into two half-ton bags, each one of which can be used to feed half as many people as the one-ton bag.[16] A good is *ex post* indivisible if the parts cannot do this. For example, two halves of an airplane cannot carry any passengers. All goods that have differentiated parts and do some specific job or set of jobs are *ex post* completely

---

[16] Morroni (1992: 26) distinguishes between technical indivisibility, which we are discussing here, and economic indivisibility in which a commodity can only be purchased in some minimum size or amount, the latter being analytically similar to the integer problem discussed in the next text paragraph.

indivisible in the sense that a part of them cannot do any amount of the job that can be done by the whole.[17]

A related *ex post* indivisibility refers to the integer problem: many consumers' and producers' goods are only available in integer amounts. This may be for physical reasons. For example, a consumer can be the sole owner of one, two or three cars, but not two and a half; a producer can install one, two or three laths, but not two and a half. It may also be for economic or customary reasons in that commodities that are physically divisible can only be purchased in discreet amounts, such as a bag of flour. Handling such issues in consumer and producer theory, as opposed to the usual assumption that all such items can be varied continuously, poses some formidable technical problems but does not affect anything that is at issue here. (For a full treatment and an extensive bibliography, see Bobzin (1998).)

2.3.2 Ex ante Divisibility and Indivisibility

This refers to altering the size of a capital good or whole plant, making a new one that is larger or smaller than the original one but that can do the same type of job. Size is a multi-dimensional concept but the essence of what is at issue can be seen by defining size in terms of capacity to do some job. For example, a truck that can carry two tons of bulk cargo is smaller than a truck that can carry four tons, but larger than one that can carry only one ton. A drill press that can drill holes in a one-inch-thick piece sheet metal at a rate of one hole per 10 seconds is smaller than one that can do the job in 5 seconds, and larger than one that takes 20 seconds to do the job. Also a factory that can produce some product at a rate of 100 items per day is larger than one that can produce the same product at a rate of 50 per day and smaller than one that can produce at a rate of 200 per day.

---

[17] Although a person is *ex post* physically indivisible, the existence of part-time hiring makes one person divisible as far as a firm is concerned. Although the same is true for some types of capital goods and some firms, for the most part a firm cannot hire part time a factory or single parts of an integrated production facility.

An Indivisible Plant

Two distinct versions of *ex ante* plant divisibility and plant indivisibility are found in the literature. In the first, a production process, plant in our terminology, is divisible if it can be scaled upward or downward by multiplying all of the inputs in its production function by some positive constant, λ, and have its output change in the same proportion. The process is defined to be indivisible in the downward direction if the result is to alter output by some multiple, γ, where $0 \leq \gamma < \lambda$. This, of course, is how constant returns and decreasing returns to scale are normally defined. Note that all of the plants that give rise to the cost curves shown in Figure 1 are indivisible in that sense. If they were not, there would be no need to accept a higher unit cost than c_1 by scaling downwards the plant that has the cost curve shown as $SRATC_5$. Analogous comments apply to each smaller sized plant down to the one with the cost curve $SRATC_1$. We call these *ncrs*-indivisibilities for non-constant returns to scale indivisibilities.

In the second version, a plant is defined as *ex ante* divisible if a smaller version can be made to do the same type of job as the larger version. In terms of Figure 1, this is the case with plants whose short-run cost curves are between $SRATC_5$ and $SRATC_2$. If the production process that has the short-run cost curve $SRATC_1$ is the smallest size plant that can produce the product in question, that production process is *ex ante* indivisible at that size. We call this an *mps*-indivisibility for minimum possible size. Note that all of the plants shown in the figure are both *ex post* indivisible and *ex ante ncrs*-indivisible, while only the smallest possible version is *ex ante mps*-indivisible (because no smaller version can be made) while all larger versions are *ex ante* divisible (because smaller versions can be made).[18]

---

[18] In the Eaton-Lipsey paper cited earlier the authors describe the services embodied in capital goods as an endogenous 'lumpiness' or 'indivisibility'. To see the problem it is necessary to distinguish, as they do not do, between lumpiness and indivisibility. Lumpiness is a variable measured in the simplest cases by the amount of services embodied in a capital good. As their argument shows, lumpiness is an endogenously determined variable. In contrast,

Two cases in which it is possible to build a plant smaller than the one with $SRATC_1$ need to be considered. In one case, the plant is technically inefficient in the sense that it uses more of all inputs for all common production levels than does the plant with the $SRATC_1$ curve.[19] In the other case, although for common production levels the plant uses fewer of some inputs than used in $SRATC_1$, it uses so much more of others that the total short-run costs always exceed those of the larger plant. So, in both cases, the cost curve of the smaller plant lies wholly above $SRATC_1$, as does the dotted curve $SRATC_0$ in Figure 3 on page 41. So, in both cases the plant that has the short-run cost curve $SRATC_1$ is producing at the lowest technically and/or economically efficient scale. For subsequent analysis it is convenient to confine ourselves to the case in which the process that gives rise to $SRATC_1$ is the smallest size that will do the job technically and economically. However, if either of the other two cases is possible the analysis is the same because curves such as $SRATC_0$ are irrelevant and can be ignored.

An Indivisible Capital Good

In the case of a capital good there is no parallel to the ncrs concept of the indivisibility of a plant. As already observed, reduction of the inputs that go to make capital goods by some constant proportion λ will probably not produce anything useful. In our three-dimensional world with its physical laws making a smaller version of some machine never requires scaling all of its inputs down in proportion.

indivisibility is a characteristic, not a variable. A thing is either divisible or it is not. The capital goods to which they refer have various amounts of lumpiness and almost all are *ex post* indivisible. But they are not *ex ante* indivisible since they are being produced with different amounts of capacity. Scale effects related to the design of capital goods are incentives to embody lumpiness in capital goods; but they do not cause *ex post* indivisibility, which is determined by the nature of most capital goods no matter how many services they do or do not embody. This is not, however, a serious problem for Eaton and Lipsey's main argument about endogenous lumpiness since all references to 'indivisibilities' can be replaced by 'lumpiness' without affecting their argument.

[19] This is doubtless an unusual case but not an inconceivable one because it often takes a lot of capital to miniaturise various processes and may take no less (or even more) labour to operate them than their large counterpart.

However, the second concept does apply. Note, that almost all capital goods that do some specific job can be made in different sizes. For example, Dudley Jackson in his piece cited below notes 288 cases in which machines that do some given job have been made of indifferent sizes and their relative efficiencies measured. Undoubtedly, there will be some smallest size of that machine that will be capable of doing its job. The machine is *ex ante* indivisible at that size. There are, however, two further possibilities in this case. First, there may be some other less specialised machines and labour that will do the same job at a smaller scale but less efficiently per unit of output. Second, there may be no alternative process to deliver the needed service and the smallest possible machine must be installed and underutilised as output falls below what it needed to employ that machine at full capacity. In this case although the machine itself is subject to an *ex ante* indivisibility, its services need not be. So the explanation of the higher cost at a lower scale of output lies not in the service flow being subject to an inequality. In this matter, there is an ambiguity in the literature in that sometimes the service flow of the capital good and at other times the good itself is shown in the PF. If it is the service of the machine that is the variable in the plant's PF, this input is continually variable downwards in the short run by operating the machine below its full capacity. Unit total costs will then rise since the capital cost of the machine does not fall when its use is reduced and must be spread over fewer units as output falls. So although the source of the scale effect is on the production side, it is not seen in the plant's PF where one of the (continuously variable) inputs is the services of this capital good; it is only seen in the cost function as some costs stay constant as the machine is used less intensively. Indeed, it is not easy to think of processes where the services of some *ex ante* indivisible capital good cannot be reduced continually either by leaving the good idle part time or disposing of its services for uses other than in the production of the good in question. In this case, although the contribution of the machine's service to unit variable costs will be constant right down to zero output, the average total cost will rise as the fixed cost of the indivisible machine is spread over fewer and fewer units of output.

2.3.3   Which Variable: A Stock or a Flow?

In Section 1 we discussed several problems associated with the specification of the variables in the production function. The above discussion reveals a further problem. Most writers when defining a PF formally state that its variables are the service flows of the various factors of production: for example, the machine hours used from some specific machine. As already mentioned, the service flow from some specific machine, or whole plant, can be reduced continually to zero by under using it, while the capital good itself cannot be so varied. So if there is an indivisibility it is related to the capital good not to its service flow. It seems implicit in the writings of those who use this explanation of scale effects that they are referring to capital goods that are, in our terminology, *ex ante* indivisible. Yet although this indivisibility may explain rising unit cost as output is reduced, it does not explain why the full services of the capital good must be used, even when production is reduced (as is implied by the minimum constraint on its use). It would seem that writers, having specified the capital good's services as the inputs in the production function, then slip into using the good itself, which clearly *is* subject to a minimum constraint on its size when it reaches the point of *ex ante* indivisibility.

2.3.4   Indivisibilities as Sources

If we look at the cost curves for alternative-sized plants shown in Figure 3, we see economies of scale over the output range from zero to q_3 and diseconomies from q_3 at least up to q_4. We require an explanation of these different relations, which implies that we need something that is present over one of these ranges and absent, or at least behaving differently, over the other range. Can indivisibilities provide such an explanation?

Ex post *Indivisibilities*

First consider *ex post* indivisibilities. All capital goods with differentiated parts, including the plants that give rise to each of the short-run cost curves SRATC$_1$ to SRATC$_8$ in Figure 3, are *ex post*

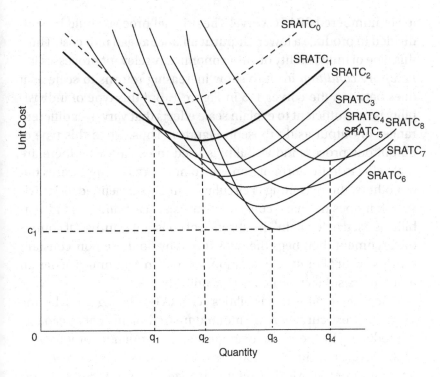

Figure 3 *Ex post* and *ex ante* indivisibilities

indivisible; you cannot cut them up and expect them to do any job, let alone the job done by the whole. Thus, this universal characteristic of all capital goods with differentiated parts cannot explain the different scale effects over different ranges of output.

Ex ante *Indivisibility of a Plant*

Now consider the *ex ante* indivisibility of a whole plant. We first take the case of *ncrs*-indivisibilities. Since each of the plants with the cost curves shown in the figure are *ex ante ncrs*-indivisible, this universal characteristic of plants that lie behind the U-shaped LRATC curve cannot explain the varying slope of that curve. If any of the processes that gave rise to any of the SRATC curves numbered 1–5 in Figure 1 were divisible in this sense, it would never be necessary to produce with a process that gave rise to a lower numbered SRATC curve. The original process could be sub-divided to produce a lower output at an unchanged unit cost. Thus, this type of indivisibility of any economically relevant processes is a *necessary condition* for it to show increasing returns to scale as it does between the curves 1–5 in Figure 1. But this type of indivisi-bility is not sufficient to explain scale effects that vary over different ranges of output as do those in Figure 1. Thus, when this type of ubiquitous process indivisibility is used to explain why there are scale effects in the form of non-constant returns in some cases but not others, the reasoning is circular: a process is defined as indivi-sible if it does not have constant returns to scale and this indivisi-bility is used to 'explain' the absence of constant returns. Of course, the argument then begs the question: Why do these non-constant returns occur? For the explanation, we look to economies of design that are the subject of the next section.

To consider *mps*-indivisibilities let $SRATC_1$ in Figure 3 be the short-run cost curve for the minimum-sized plant that is capable of producing the commodity in question, the quantity produced at its MES is q_2. For simplicity, we assume that the size of the plant can only be raised above that minimum size in discrete amounts, as shown by the various SRATC curves in the figure.[20] Since there is no relevant SRATC curve associated with a smaller sized plant, the LRAC curve follows this short-run $SRATC_1$ curve until it is inter-sected by the short-run curve associated with the next largest pos-sible sized plant which occurs at output quantity q_1 in the figure. So, for higher outputs than q_1 the LRAC curve follows the outer segment of each relevant short-run cost curve as larger and larger plants are utilised to produce larger and larger flows of production.[21] The production of this product is *ex ante* indivisible at the scale of the plant with $SRATC_1$. So, outputs from zero to q_1 are produced under

---

[20] Hirshleifer et al. (2005: 177) mention this case in which the fixed factor can only be varied in discrete amounts.

[21] As noted earlier, if we assume that plant size can be varied by smaller and smaller increments beyond the plant with cost curve $SRATC_1$, we get, in the limit, the standard smooth LRAC curve which is the envelop of these tightly packed short run cost curves.

conditions of falling unit costs because of this *ex ante* indivisibility of the plant. This minimum-sized plant is sufficient to cause economies of scale as it determines the LRAC curve, but only up to an output of q_1, after which this *mps*-indivisibility is irrelevant as plants larger than this minimum size are being employed.

Ex ante *Indivisibility of an Individual Capital Good*

Now consider *ex ante mps*-indivisibility of an individual capital good. In the first case that we consider there are other less specialised machines and labour that can deliver the same service. Although the indivisibility of the machine is a necessary condition for a switch to a less efficient process to deliver the needed service, the explanation of the scale effect is in the reasons for the different efficiencies of the two processes, which lie in economies of design, not in the indivisibility of the more specialised machine.

In the second case, the machine is indivisible and has no smaller substitutes. For example, let there be a machine that is used at all scales of production up q_4 and let it be *ex ante mps*-indivisible at a size whose full employment comes with the output at the minimum unit cost on the curve SRATC$_4$. Now for lower outputs this machine will not be fully utilised. So, when output increases from zero to where the machine is fully employed, there will be downward pressure on unit cost as a result of the spreading of the machine's fixed cost. This will be in addition to all of the reasons for falling unit cost due to economies of design as the larger and larger plants are built with MESs from q_1 to q_4.

What if one production process uses several such machines? According to Morroni (1992: 28), in this case 'to avoid using individual machines at sub-optimal levels the overall scale of the production unit must be equal to the lowest common multiple of the productive capacity of the individual machines'. If there are several such machines, each with its own different capacity, this could be quite a large number. But Morroni only considers *ex post* indivisibility and so does not ask: what if different versions of these machines can be made each with a different capacity? At the extreme, if all can be made with continually varying sizes and capacities down to some minimum *mps*-indivisibility, then this sub-capacity effect will only be felt below the minimum capacity of the largest machine. All other machines will be made with sizes that match the desired capacity of that machine.

Exactly how important this effect of *ex ante mps*-indivisibility of individual machines in plants that are larger than the minimum possible plant size compared to the importance of economies of design is a matter that cannot be decided without empirical evidence.

2.3.5   Interesting Exceptions

There are some interesting exceptions to the frequent existence of *ex ante mps*-indivisibilities of capital goods. These are goods for which there is no relevant finite minimum size needed to do the type of job in question. Interestingly, this includes pipe lines that are often quoted as examples of indivisibilities. Of course, as with all capital goods with differentiated parts, pipe lines are *ex post* indivisible. But they are not *ex ante* indivisible. They can be made as short as needed, depending on the space over which a liquid is to be transferred, and they can be made with as small a radius as is needed, depending on the required rate of liquid transfer. Similarly, the fenced pasture studied in the previous section is not *ex ante* indivisible. Of course, like virtually all other capital goods both of these are *ex post* indivisible, if cut in half once built, they cannot do their jobs. But they can be made *ex ante* as small as required, down to one square inch of fenced pasture and a one foot long narrow pipe. So, the economies of scale associated with pipe lines, fences, and other similar capital goods, extend over the whole range of their outputs from zero to an indefinitely large size and have nothing to do with *ex ante* indivisibilities, which are non-existent.

2.3.6   Summary: Indivisibilities as Valid Sources of Scale Effects

As we have observed, any valid explanation of EoS effects must be able to explain why these occur only over some range of output, such as is shown in Figure 1. *Ex post* indivisibilities cannot do this because they occur at all levels of output for any capital good with differentiated parts. Neither is the absence of constant returns to scale an explanation, as explained above in the section 'ex ante

Indivisibility of a Plant'. It is a necessary but not a sufficient condition for scale effects. The only valid explanation that we have found is the *ex ante mps*-indivisibility in that there is some smallest version of a plant or individual machine that is necessary to produce some product or capital service. As output varies over the smallest version from zero to that unit's capacity, scale effects are encountered. But as soon as it is economic to use a larger version of that plant or capital good, *ex ante* invisibilities are no longer an explanation of what is observed. It follows that we need to look to economies of design (and a few other minor sources that we considered later) for an explanation of the majority of the observed scale effects.

2.3.7 Indivisibilities in the Literature

Because of the major difference between the assessments of the importance of indivisibilities found in the literature and the present treatment, it is important to survey all of the authors in our list of references who wrote about the definition of the indivisibilities and then stated that they were sources of scale effects. Of course, given the various meanings of indivisibility that are distinguished here, and given that most authors do not make such distinctions, there is a certain ambiguity in many of these quotations. Nonetheless, over all they serve to show the variety of different views on how indivisibilities may cause scale effects – many of which are contradicted by the above analysis.

Ex post *Divisibility and Indivisibility*

Some authors seem to rely on *ex post* indivisibility to explain scale effects, something that we have seen is invalid given that it is a universal characteristic of all goods with differentiated parts.

> I have not found one example of increasing returns to scale in which there is not *some indivisible commodity* in the surrounding circumstances. The oft-quoted case of a pipeline whose diameter is a continuous variable ... [requires] one entire pipeline of the requisite length ... to render the service. Half the length of line does not carry half the flow of oil. (Koopmans 1957: 152 fn. 3, italics added)

Assume for instance that the only input is some specific capital good (a machine, plant, ship or pipeline) which is indivisible in the sense that it becomes useless if physically divided.   (Silvestre 1987: 2799)

Frequently, an economy of scale results simply from the fact that a certain factor of production is indivisible, that is, it cannot be divided into smaller units.   (Ammer & Ammer 1984: 415)

What is being illustrated in Table A.7 is the feature of discontinuous production changes arising from indivisibilities. In other words, certain production processes involving, say, very lumpy capital equipment can only be operated if the scale is B or C. More to the point it is not possible to halve the equipment and operate it at a lower scale, because different processes have different unit levels of operation. This implies that even in the long run factors are not perfectly divisible.   (Shone 1981: 156)

Although somewhat ambiguous, Shone appears to be referring to *ex post* indivisibility.

According to Morroni, technical indivisibility 'refers to the impossibility of dividing a particular commodity once it is exchanged, into [smaller] amounts usable for production or consumption.[*ex post* indivisibility]' (1992: 26) This is not to be 'confused with the possibility of exchanging a given commodity available in continuously increasing size [*ex ante* indivisibility]'. (1992: 26) 'Most fund elements [capital goods] are indivisible.' (1992: 25) Having explicitly ruled out *ex ante* indivisibility, he gets scale effects by the spreading of overheads when the capital good is used at less than capacity which as we have noted is a valid explanation when the good is *ex ante mps*-indivisible but not when it is made to any larger size. Thus, his analysis does not explain scale effects for a firm larger than the one with SRATC$_1$ in Figure 3. It is unclear, however, that he intends to restrict the influence of indivisibilities to such minimum-sized plants since he has explicitly defined indivisibilities *ex post* and ruled out *ex ante mps*-indivisibilities.[22]

---

[22] In another place Morroni seems to define indivisibilities as *ex ante ncrs*-indivisibilities, '[a] process is indivisible if it is impossible to activate processes

Other authors refer to our *ex ante* indivisibility and then use as an illustration the *ex post* indivisibility that applies to all goods with differentiated parts.

Indivisibilities: Some inputs just do not come in small units [*ex ante* indivisibility?]. We cannot install half a blast furnace or half a locomotive (a small locomotive is not the same as a fraction of a large locomotive). [*ex post* indivisibility] As a result, only if operations are carried out on a sufficiently large scale will it pay to employ such indivisible units.   (Baumol 1977: 274)

'[I]f a firm doubles its scale, it may be able to use techniques that could not be used at the smaller scale. Some inputs are not available in small units; for example, we cannot install half an open hearth furnace [*ex post* indivisibility]. Because of indivisibilities of this sort, increasing returns to scale may occur.'   (Mansfield 1979: 142)

But of course you can have open hearth furnaces of various sizes. Only the minimum possible size is *ex ante* indivisible.

'[Indivisibilities are defined as] the minimum physical or technical size limitations on FACTOR INPUTS. For example, a company wants to purchase a machine that can undertake 5,000 operations a day. Because of design and technical difficulties, the minimum-size machine available optimally carries out 10,000 operations a day. The machine is indivisible since it cannot be reduced to two optimal half-machines'   (Pass et al. 2005: 251).

Is not clear what is being referred to here but it seems that the penultimate sentence refers to *ex ante* indivisibility and the final one to *ex post* indivisibility.

Indivisibility, or discontinuity, the technical or physical characteristics of a factor of production or commodity which prevents its being used except in minimum quantities [meaning unclear]. Most machinery and capital equipment must be used in 'lumps' of

that have the same proportions of inputs and outputs, but on a smaller scale' (Morroni 1992: 145 note 4).

minimum size. A workman is also an 'indivisible' unit in this respect; the hands used for an assembly line cannot be separated from the legs that could be simultaneously used for messenger work [this appears to refer to *ex post* indivisibilities]. ... [A]t some scales of production it may pay a firm to have a market research department or a staff training school. Where the size of the indivisible unit is large (in relation to annual output) plants or firms will tend to be large: technical indivisibilities tend to determine the size of the plant; other, such as financial, the size of the firms [this appears to be referring to *ex ante mps*-indivisibilities]. (Seldon & Pennance 1976: 181)

Yet other authors are unclear if *ex ante* or *ex post* indivisibilities are responsible for scale effects.

'indivisibilities: A production factor that cannot be segregated further into smaller elements. The input variable is restricted in some way by size' (Shim & Siegal 1995: 182).

It is unclear if this refers to *ex ante* or *ex post* indivisibility.

'Indivisibilities: The impossibility of dividing a factor into smaller units' (Sloman 2006: 132).

Again it is not clear if *ex post* or *ex ante* indivisibility is being refereed to here. Elsewhere Sloman uses R&D as an example of an indivisibility, saying that 'only a large firm can set up a research laboratory' He does not, however, deal with the fact that R&D labs can be of various sizes.

Discreteness

Some of our authors argue that discreteness of an input is a source of scale effects. The clearest example of this is given by Morroni (1992) who defines economic indivisibility as occurring when 'it is impossible to exchange less than a given unit of some commodity'. This differs from his technical indivisibility because one can divide the commodity then restore it to its original size as one can divide a 2 kilogram bag of flour into two one kilo bags and then restore the contexts to one 2 kilo bag, which cannot be done by dividing the recombining the typical machine. If inputs must be purchased in large units, inventories of them must be held as they are used up over time. This confers an economy of scale as output is increased so allowing the average inventory of such commodities to be reduced.

The other author in our survey who mentions this effect is Rutherford (2000: 220) who writes: 'The nature of a factor of production or commodity which is only supplied in discrete amounts, not increasing or decreasing in quantity continuously.' He goes on to say: 'Indivisibilities are responsible for many fixed costs in the short run and give rise to production economies of scale at high levels of output.'

Ex ante *Indivisibility and the Absence of Constant Returns to Scale*

A few authors define *ex ante* indivisibility as the absence of constant returns to scale as production is decreased. But to define indivisibility as the absence of constant return of scale for decreases in output and then argue that indivisibilities explain non-constant returns is circular reasoning. The only author in our survey to note this is Morroni who writes (1992: 144-5): 'the assertion often found in the literature that . . . increasing returns to scale depend on indivisibility, is a tautology'.

> Indivisibilities: Certain processes of production . . . can only be operated efficiently at large output volumes and cannot be operated as efficiently at lower outputs, even if all factor inputs are scaled down in proportion to one another. We call this inability to scale down the processes of production without affecting their efficiency of operation, indivisibility of the production process.
>
> (Griffiths & Wall 2000: 170)

These authors list indivisibilities as a source of scale effects and so seem to be involved in the circular reasoning just discussed.

> 'Divisibility: Output from any process can be expanded or contracted to any arbitrary degree by proportional expansion or contraction of all inputs used in the process'   (Quirk 1987: 145).

We can infer that indivisibility is defined as the absence of the above condition. The author does not, however, link indivisibilities so defined to scale effects.

The proportionality postulate states: 'if an activity $a = (a_1, a_2, \ldots, a_n)$ is possible, then every activity $\lambda a = (\lambda a_1, \lambda a_2, \ldots, \lambda a_n)$ of which the net outputs are proportional to those of a, with a non-negative proportionality factor, λ, is also possible' (Koopmans 1957: 76). He goes on to state that a (process) indivisibility occurs when one or more of the a_is cannot be varied continuously, particularly if it is subject of an inequality constraint: $a_i \geq \bar{a}_i$. This is not the circular reasoning of the others who define indivisibilities as the absence of a constant-returns PF, but a statement that indivisibility occurs when one of the variables in the constant-returns PF cannot be altered in proportion to the others, or in the limit, not altered at all. Koopmans is the only author in our survey who appears to believe that all scale effects are due to indivisibilities as he defines them.[23]

Having originally agreed with Koopmans that all cases of increasing returns to scale were due to indivisibilities, Kaldor (1972: 102–3) later recanted and argued that there were other reasons for scale effects such as geometrical relations, and also that Koopmans' concept of indivisible inputs was misleading. On this he wrote: 'There is nothing "indivisible" about tubes or pipelines as such, technically, it may be just as easy to make tubes of a relatively small or a relatively large dimension there can be a continuous range of sizes in between.' Although he does not use our terms, Kaldor is clearly chiding Koopmans for using an *ex post* rather than an *ex ante* definition in his pipeline example.

---

[23] Notice that this appears to deduce an empirical proposition – scale effects can only result from indivisibilities – from a highly abstracted formulation of a production function in which all that appears is the flow of services from the various inputs, including capital goods, but not the goods themselves that are subject to the alleged indivisibilities. The correct deduction is not that scale effects can only result from an indivisibility of inputs, but that this abstract formulation has removed all possible sources of scale effects other than those that are associated with some characteristic of the input flows, of which indivisibility is the obvious candidate.

It is not quite clear how to categorise the rather odd treatment by Bannock et al. (1984: 141, bracketed numbers added):

> Indivisibilities: Many types of plant and machinery have, for engineering reasons, a single most efficient size. Either [1] it will be technically impossible to make the equipment at a different size, or [2] the production costs associated with other sizes are higher.... Certain types of production processes may only be viable at certain rates of output. The word indivisibilities is used to categorize these sources of scale economies because [3] they would not arise if the plant and processes were capable of being increased or decreased in scale by small amounts without any change in their nature, i.e. if they were perfectly divisible.

The point numbered (1) refers to a (unlikely) form of *ex ante* indivisibility in that the machine can only be made to one size while (2) seems to explain scale efficiencies by themselves in the sense that the variations in unit cost as size varies is not an indivisibility but a result of some other factor that causes scale effects. Entry (3) correctly points out that *ncrs*-indivisibilities are a necessary condition for EoS to occur.[24]

Ex ante *Divisibility and Indivisibility of a Capital Good*

Finally, we come to the use of the term in the literature that seems to apply to the type of *ex ante* indivisibility that we have argued is the only type of indivisibility that can explain variable scale effects. Unambiguous statements to that effect follow.

'A commodity is indivisible if it has a minimum size below which it is unavailable, at least without significant qualitative change' (Baumol 2008: 242). Compare this with Baumol (1977) cited above and note that the last qualification 'without...' is ambiguous.

---

[24] Bannock et al., also quote the division of labour as a kind of indivisibility: 'Expansion in scale of activities permits greater specialization and division of labour among workers ... This, in effect, is also an "indivisibility", in that it is the result of the fixed capacity of individual worker and the fact that it is optimally utilized when devoted exclusively to a specific task' (1984: 141).

Indivisibilities are defined as 'the existence of a minimum scale at which any technique can operate. This applies to all productive techniques' (Black et al. 2012: 204). I presume they mean 'operate at full capacity' as most techniques can operate below full capacity, which is the range of increasing returns for the firm with the curve $SRATC_1$ in Figure 1.

'A commodity is indivisible if it has a minimum size below which it is unavailable'   (Calhoun 2002: 229).

'[I]ndivisibilities: the minimum physical or technical size limitations of factor inputs'. 'Economies of scale may ... arise due to: (a) indivisibilities in machinery and equipment especially where a number of processes are linked together'

(Pass et al. 2005: 251 and 156).

'The characteristic of a factor of production or commodity which prevents its use below a certain minimum level' (Pearce 1992: 201). The qualification 'use' is odd here because, as already mentioned, equipment can be, and frequently is, used at less than full capacity. Presumably this refers to the machine that produces the service that is the factor of production. The machine comes in some minimum size (*ex ante* indivisibility) but not the service input. This is yet another example of the ambiguities that enter because of the failure to consider explicitly two-stage production processes so that the machine that produces a service input is confused with the input itself.

'Consider a production process that requires constant input proportions and yields constant returns to scale. Two persons and two shovels can do twice as much as one person with one shovel; but we cannot have half a person with half a shovel; consequently, we have an indivisibility in the production process' (Miller 1978: 458). Presumably one person and one shovel is assumed to be the minimum *ex ante* size that can do the digging job (no part time work or hiring of the services of the shovel for less than full time).

Examples of indivisibilities are the cost of designing and developing a product, such as an aircraft, car or computer programme, setting up a production line for a product or for a batch of a product, the capacity of a machine and a TV advert. A firm that cannot fully utilize the item to which the indivisible cost relates, or spread its cost over as large an output as its rivals, is at a disadvantage. However, it may be able to damp down its cost disadvantage by, for example, acquiring a second-hand machine tool, or by using a different type of promotion in place of TV advertising.   (Pratten 2004: 283)

Although not altogether clear, this would seem to refer to *ex ante* indivisibilities while mixing once-for-all costs of product design with costs associated with the indivisibilities of production equipment.

2.3.8 Are Indivisibilities a Source of Economies of Scale or Returns to Scale?

As in most other cases, the authors who cite indivisibilities as important causes of scale effects differ in how they classify these as sources. Some list them as sources of IRTS.[25] Others say they cause both IRTS and EoS.[26] Many others list them as sources of EoS only.[27] Finally, Eaton and Lipsey (1977) argue that indivisibilities are the key to explaining why production is located at points in space rather than being spread evenly at points of consumption. If we add *ex ante* to their term 'indivisibilities' this attribution is satisfactory.

---

[25] These are Kamerschen and Valentine (1977: 179) and Koopmans (1957: 76).

[26] These are Griffiths and Wall (2000: 170), Bannock et al. (1984: 141), Setterfield (2001: 489), Carlaw and Lipsey (2008a: 222), Seldon and Pennance (1976: 120, 295) and Pass et al. (2005: 156, 475).

[27] These are Ammer and Ammer (1984: 415), Bain (1968: 492), Baumol (1977: 274), Black et al. (2012: 123, 204), Brush (1994: 339), Calhoun (2002: 229), Pearce (1992: 201), Silvestre (1987: 2797), Rutherford (2000: 220), Sloman (2006: 132) and Graaff (1987: 7599).

2.4   Scale Effects Due of Geometry and Physical Laws

Several key characteristics of our world are important for understanding the pervasiveness of scale effects related to the design effects of reconfiguring capital goods. One source of these is the world's three dimensionality. For example, the volume of any regular container increases more than in proportion to the materials needed to make up its sides. Another source is our world's physical laws where nonlinear effects also abound. For example, the observed intensity of a light is inversely proportional to the square of the distance from the light source. Yet another source is the stochastic nature of many aspects of our world's behaviour. For example, if the probability of one event happening is $1/r$ ($1 < r$), then the probability of n such events happening at the same time, but independently of each other, is $1/r^n$, which is diminishing non-linearly in n.

So, when we change the scale of almost anything, from one machine to a whole plant or skyscraper, we should, as have already observed in the introduction, expect to encounter scale effects of the sort that we call design effects and for these pervasive reasons alone – and there are other causes as well. These effects should be no surprise; the only surprises should occur if we encounter no scale effects when the scale of any operation is changed.

2.4.1   Empirical Evidence of Design Effects
with Capital Goods

Somewhat less general than the Eaton-Lipsey treatment discussed above, but equally interesting is the treatment provided by Dudley Jackson (1996) who is one of the very few authors in our survey who introduced detailed empirical content into their discussions of scale effects. (All quotations are from pagers 229–30.) He deals with these effects at the level of individual pieces of capital equipment. Importantly, he defines scaling up in the way found in the engineering rather than the economics literature. Instead of using the returns definition of multiplying all inputs by some constant λ, one that has few if any real-world counterparts, he defines scaling up as occurring when 'each piece of equipment of smaller capacity is replaced by a piece of equipment (of the same type) but with a larger capacity'. As he puts it,

> [E]conomies of scale refers to the situation in which, at a given and unchanging set of input prices, the unit cost of production is lower in a plant of larger scale of (annual) output than in a plant of smaller scale. This happens because the physical requirement for labour and capital inputs per unit of output each tends to be lower the larger is the scale of annual output which the plant is designed to produce.

Clearly he is referring to somethings close to, but not identical with, what the literature calls IRTS, which of course, given constant input prices, leads to EoS. He then defines the power rule as:

> Let K denote the acquisition cost of a piece of equipment and V ... [its] capacity (however measured); the subscripts i and j denote, respectively, pieces of equipment of the same type but different capacity, i being the larger capacity and ... let s denote a parameter of the power rule ... $K_i/K_j = (V_i/V_j)^s$.

He goes on to argue that for economists 'the interest of such data lies in the value of s for each type of equipment; nearly always less than one and centering around approximately 2/3. For example, in a sample of 288 types of equipment the average value of s was 0.6559 (with a standard deviation of 0.2656)'. Thus, a doubling of capacity of some generic capital good increases its cost on average by about two-thirds. He concludes that 'economies of scale is a widespread and inherent feature of the behaviour of the acquisition cost of equipment or of a plant as capacity is "scaled up" '.

This is strong evidence of the pervasiveness of scale effects related to individual pieces of capital equipment. This even though he uses a different definition of IRTS than is found in the economics literature, one that applies where it is possible to build different sized versions of what is basically the same type of capital equipment. Note, however, that when the scale of operations is increased, building a larger set of capital goods to do the same range of jobs is not always optimal behaviour compared with reorganising the whole production process using quite different equipment.

2.4.2   Sources of Design Effects: Geometry and Physics

As already observed, we live in a three-dimensional world that entails many scale effects, both increasing and diminishing. For example, the geometrical relation governing any container typically makes the amount of material used, and hence its cost, proportional to *one dimension less than* the service output, giving increasing returns to scale with respect to the inputs of materials over the whole range of output. For example, the capacity of a closed cubic container of sides s is s^3. The amount of material required for construction is $6s^2$. So, material required per unit of capacity is $6/s$, which is diminishing in s, indicating IRTD. Also, the total amount of welding required to seal the sides of the container is proportional to the total length of the seams, which is $12s$, or $12/s^2$ per unit of capacity. So not only does both the amount of materials and the cost of sealing the seams fall per unit of capacity as the capital good's capacity is increased, they fall at different rates. This relation holds for more than just storage containers. Blast furnaces, ships, gasoline engines, office and residential buildings are a few examples of the myriad technologies that show such geometrical scale effects.

   The geometrical reasoning given above cannot produce a final conclusion about scale effects related to containers; one needs to know some physics as well. It is imaginable, for example, that as the capacity of a container is increased, the walls would need to be thickened proportionally, making the volume of material increase linearly with the container's capacity. Physical relations dictate that in most cases this is not so. Although some thickening is often required, in many cases, the thickening is less than in proportion to the increase in the surface area. Then the volume of material used increases less than in proportion to the increase in capacity (although more than in proportion to the increase in surface area). In either case, the returns depend on the technical relations that govern each case in question.

To make an old fashioned light bulb last longer, what is required is to alter the strength of the filament without a proportionate change in most of its other components. Similarly, to make a light bulb deliver a larger wattage of light per unit of time, what is needed is to change the resistance of the filament with no change in the other components. This gives IRTD that occur when either the duration or rate of flow of the services of the light bulb are varied over a wide range of duration and wattage. This example generalises to the large number of technologies in which the flow or intensity of its service is a function of only part of the device.[28] In all such cases there is in effect a spreading of overheads as the parts that do not require alteration have falling cost per unit of output as the technology is changed.

There are many scale effects associated with ships, some depending on geometrical relations and others on physical laws. First, the maximum speed that a displacement hull can be driven through the water is proportional to the square root of the length of the hull on the water line (planing hulls obey different laws) (Hiscock 1965: 138). No amount of *a priori* reasoning could reveal this rather mysterious relation. Second, while a ship's carrying capacity is roughly proportional to the cube of its length on the water line, geometrical relations plus the physics governing structural strength of a hollow body dictate that the ship's cost is related approximately linearly to its water line length (Rosenberg & Birdzell 1986: 83). Third, altering the ship's size also alters its handling and safety characteristics in complex ways. Fourth, as the size and other characteristics of a ship are changed, there is an alteration in the materials best used for its construction. Finally, the amount of horsepower per ton of cargo required to move the ship through the water, changes as the size of the ship changes, falling over a wide range as size increases. Thus, building larger ships alters carrying capacity, construction costs, operating costs,

---

[28] Indeed, all that is needed is that the output be differently related to the various parts of the device, not that the relation be zero for variations over a minimum necessary amount for some parts and a given positive number for the others.

speed and other handling characteristics, each in a different proportion.

The cost per passenger mile for airplanes falls steadily as the size of the aircraft is increased over a wide range of sizes. Also, there is an improvement in its stability in the face of turbulent conditions and in several other handling characteristics. Analogous considerations cause many scale effects in land transport – again in response to both geometrical properties and physical laws.

According to the physics of heat, the heat loss from a blast furnace is proportional to the area of its surface, while the amount of ore that can be smelted is proportional to the cube of the surface sides. This relation will be considered in more detail in Section 5 and is a source of increasing returns in the relation between fuel used and output capacity of such furnaces. Once again, the relation arises from a combination of the physics and geometry of our world. (Since the time of Isaac Newton, practical engineers have known that a small body loses heat faster than a large body. See, for example, Cardwell (1995: 158).)

As with blast furnaces, the heat loss from a steam engine's cylinder is proportional to the cylinder's surface area while the power it generates is proportional to the volume of the cylinder. This is one of the several reasons why the thermal efficiency of a steam engine is an increasing function of its size over a wide range starting from zero. This in turn is why steam powered factories were built much larger than the water powered factories that they displaced. There are no similar scale effects with electric motors (beyond a very small size), which is one reason why small-scale parts manufacturers (feeding into large-scale assemblers) became efficient when electricity replaced steam as the major power source for manufacturing. Also, when the absence of significant scale effects allowed unit-drive machines (one motor per machine) to replace machines driven by belts emanating from a central drive shift driven by a single large steam engine, a more rational arrangement of the machines in the factory became possible. This in combination with new machine tools that could cut pre-hardened steel, eventually led to the introduction of the assembly line with its massive scale economies – a development that would not have been possible in steam-powered factories. Although these changes took place over time and so were another example of what Lipsey, Carlaw and Bekar (2005) call historical returns to scale (see Section 5), they illustrate the influence at any one time of scale effects on the general economy. Each of these technologies was associated with a given and different set of scale effects, so each influenced in different ways the current organisation of firms and industries and also had important effects on productivity.

The Literature

Although none of our surveyed authors refer to physical laws, many mention geometrical properties as a source of scale effects. We have already mentioned the important material on the magnitude and scope of scale effects in machinery cited by Dudley Jackson (1996), effects that he attributes to the geometrical properties of machinery. Of the rest, Sloman (2006: 132) says more about geometrical effects than most of the others in our survey. He refers to the 'container principle', which he says is a source of IRTS and EoS at the plant level: 'Any capital equipment that contains things (blast furnaces, oil tankers, pipes, vats, etc.) tends to cost less per unit of output the larger its size. The reason has to do with the relationship between a container's volume and its surface area.' His comments might be seen as implying geometrical sources more generally, although all of the examples he cites are applications of his 'container principle', while as we have seen above, there are causes that rely on geometrical properties other than the container principle. Carlaw and Lipsey (2008a: 222) list spatial facts about the world (e.g. surface area-volume relationships) as causes of IRTS in capital goods which lead to EoS for the final goods producers that use them. Jackson (1996: 230) argues that spatial relations such as that between surface area and volume are the most important source of EoS in the process of 'scaling up' production facilities. Pass et al. (2005: 156) list under the heading EoS 'economies of increased dimensions for many types of capital equipment (e.g. tankers, boilers) both set-up and operating costs increase less rapidly than capacity'. Bannock et al. (1984: 141) refer to the volume effect in general and shipping in particular as sources of both IRTS and EoS. Setterfield (2001: 488) and Miller (1978: 208) also mention geometry as causes of both. Baumol (1977: 274) lists them under a returns section but in places refers to them as economies, while Griffiths and Wall (2000: 171), Kamerschen and Valentine (1977: 185), Quirk (1987: 149) and Varian (1992: 15) call them sources of IRTS.

In contrast to these writers, Eatwell (2008: 140) argues as follows:

> There are some examples in which outputs are an increasing function of inputs for purely technical reasons. . . . Such technical examples are not, however, the examples which typically come to mind in the discussion of increasing returns to scale. More typical are examples of mass production, of production lines, or, today, of production integrated by means of sophisticated information systems.

One wonders if many of the examples just mentioned 'came to Eatwell's mind' only to be dismissed, or if he was unaware of them. It is symptomatic of many economists' lack of interest in the technology of the real world that Eatwell dismisses these nearly ubiquitous cases as 'purely technical', as if economics was not much concerned with the technical matters that underlie so many economic relations. One also wonders, if the scale effects associated with sophisticated information systems are not due to 'technical reasons', what mysterious non-technical reasons do account for them.[29]

2.4.3 Scale Effects Due to Random Behaviour

As already observed, we live in a world in which outcomes are often probabilistic rather than being deterministic (to say nothing of those that are genuinely uncertain). As a result, statistical relations, such as the law of large numbers, confer scale effects on many of

---

[29] Lipsey (2009: 853–4) discusses other cases in which the reluctance of many economists to be concerned with the details of relevant technologies hinders their attempts to explain important events.

our activities, effects that depend on design changes that exploit neither geometrical relations nor physical laws.

In insurance, the greater the number of independent events that are insured against, the smaller is the probability that the loss in any one year will exceed the premiums paid in that year, yielding EoS in insurance. Similar considerations apply to many other activities whose outcomes are subject to chance, such as inventories held by producers and precautionary money balances held by agents.

These examples illustrate that when the scale of output is altered in the long run, and capital is altered by reconfiguration with known technology rather than replication, the nature of the world in which we live will almost always produce a complex set of scale-related changes in the real resource cost of capital goods. Other changes will alter the capital good's performance characteristics in ways that are only indirectly reflected in the relevant service flow.

An interesting set of cases where the design of capital goods in response to probabilistic behaviour creates scale effects has been studied by Kenneth Carlaw (2004). As we have already mentioned, capital goods are commonly comprised of several distinct components that are complementary to each other. These technological complementarities, plus uncertainty about how long each component will last, create problems for designers of capital goods. To study this issue Carlaw assumes, in one of his many illustrative cases, that the probability that any one component of the capital good will be hit by a damaging stress in any one period is 0.5 and the designer of the capital good wants it to yield services for three periods at a rate of one unit of service per period. When a stress arrives, it does so at the beginning of the period, and the component delivers its services in that period only if the number of stresses it has been designed to withstand has not then been exceeded. For simplicity, he assumes a zero rate of time discount. First let a given capital good have only one component. The expected total value of services over three periods increases linearly as the component is built to withstand up to two stresses but then by a smaller amount when resilience to a third stress is added.[30] Now suppose that the good is made of two components, each with the same but independent probability (0.5) of a damaging stress occurring at the beginning of each period and that the loss of any one component renders the good useless. In this case (again assuming a zero rate of time discount) the expected value of total services increases at an increasing rate over some range as the number of stresses each component can withstand is increased.[31] So the cost-minimising designer will create durability to exploit the scale effects inherent in the nature of multiple component systems and risk of failure.

Obviously, the conditions of this example can be altered in many ways, including more periods to be served, more components liable to failure, different costs of protection against failure for each component or each additional unit of protection in any one component. However, there is no *a priori* reason to expect constant returns to design when any one of these conditions is altered.

Four of our surveyed authors mention probability issues: Bannock et al. (1984: 141) who refers to the law of large numbers so that 'the size of stocks will vary less than proportionately with the scale of output, expenditure or receipts'; Baumol (1977: 274)

---

[30] If the component is built to withstand no stresses, the probability of surviving to be used for three periods is 0.125 and the expected total services are 3(0.125) = 0.375. With the ability to withstand one stress, the probability of surviving three periods is 0.5 and the expected total services are 3(0.5) = 1.5. With the ability to withstand two stresses, the probability of surviving three periods is 0.875 and the expected total services are 3(0.875) = 2.625. With the ability to withstand three stresses, the probability of surviving three periods is 1 and the expected total services are 3.

[31] If each component is built to withstand no stresses, the probability of surviving three periods is 0.0156. With the ability of each to withstand one stress it is 0.25. With the ability to withstand two stresses it is 0.766. With the ability to withstand three stresses the probability of surviving three periods is again obviously 1. Expected total services in each case are calculated as in the previous footnote. We see in this case that there is a range of increasing returns from zero to two hits. But building the components to each withstand a third hit yields diminishing returns for this last unit of durability. Assuming a constant cost of increasing resilience to hits, the average cost curve is U-shaped.

who refers to inventories and uses both the terms returns and economies in discussing them; Carlaw and Lipsey (2008a: 222) who cite this as a source of IRTS leading to EoS; and Kamerschen and Valentine (1977: 185) who refer to the statistical law of large numbers.

2.4.4   Specialisation of Capital and Labour

One particular source of design effects, the increased specialisation of labour and capital as output rises, is quoted by many writers as a source of increasing returns to scale. Specialisation of labour and capital equipment usually go together, one requiring the other. So, we will discuss mainly the use of specialised capital as output expands. In this case labour and simple tools are replaced by specialised machines, not just larger versions of one generic machine. While in most of our surveyed literature this is merely asserted, Vassilakas presents an extended treatment calling it the major source of increasing returns to scale. He quotes Adam Smith's three reasons for this: 'First, . . . the increase of dexterity in every particular workman, secondly . . . the saving of the time which is commonly lost in passing from one species of work to another, and lastly . . . the invention of a great number of machines which facilitate and abridge labour, and enable one man to do the work of many' (as quoted by Vassilakas 1987: 4626). He then covers extensively the history of the concept since Smith's time. However, he offers no further reasons why increasing the division of labour is a source of ubiquitous scale effects; instead he confines his discussion to the circumstances under which these increasing returns are or are not exploited by firms. This is an interesting question, but not our present concern, which is the source of scale effects. If we accept Smith's reasons, we adapt his third point to our static analysis by saying: 'allowing the use of existing machines which . . .'.

Why does increased specialisation of capital goods (and the accompanying labour) typically lower unit costs? There is no fundamental overarching principle involved here. It is merely a common observation that replacing labour by specialised machines (and their specialised operators or supervisors, if there are any) often lowers unit costs because the machine can do the job faster, more precisely, with fewer errors and less variations of performance due to fatigue than can a labourer. This is often so much more efficient that the accumulated labour, materials and other costs that go to make the machine, plus the wages of its operator (if there is one), are lower per unit of output than the cost of the less specialised labour and machines that it replaces. This was the case for example when machine-operated X-rays and lasers replaced the lumber mill's experienced sawyer in determining where to make the first cut in a log. More generally it was the case when the shift of output from artisan-style to mass-production-style production when many of the things that experienced artisans did were replaced by much faster moving machines.

All of this raises the question of why the less specialised version of the production process is ever used if the more specialised version is more productive. The answer lies in the *ex ante* indivisibility of the more specialised version.

The Literature

Labour and capital specialisations are usually listed separately in the literature. Several authors state that labour specialisation causes both a returns and an economies effect unconditionally.[32] Others, argue that it is a source of both types of effect under the assumption that input prices are constant.[33] Yet others in our survey state that it is a source of EoS only.[34] Pass et al. (2005: 156,

---

[32] These are Krugman and Wells (2009: 323), Pass et al. (2005: 156, 475), Setterfield (2001: 489), Seldon and Pennance (1976: 120, 295), Pindyck and Rubinfeld (2009: 215, 245) Griffiths and Wall (2000: 171) Mansfield (1979: 185) and Bannock et al. (1984: 141). Kamerschen and Valentine (1977: 185) discuss this issue under the heading of 'returns to scale' but make statements that might can be interpreted as meaning economies as well.

[33] These are Perloff (2012: 172), McConnell et al. (2012: 154), Sloman (2006: 132) and Parkin et al. (2005: 195, 214).

[34] These are Ammer and Ammer (1984: 415), Bain (1968: 492), Mankiw (2006: 274) Abraham-Frois (2008: 232), Bannock et al. (2003: 114) Black et al. (2012: 123), Farrell (1997: 432) and Shim and Siegal (1995: 118).

475) appear to argue incorrectly that the presence of an EoS implies that of an IRTS (while, as we have seen, the latter implies the former, the former does not imply the later).[35]

Several writers also cite managerial specialisation as a separate source of scale effects, although there would seem to be no obvious analytical difference between white and blue collar specialisation. Some list it as a source of both IRTS and EoS, sometimes with and sometimes without the qualification of fixed input prices, while yet others list it as a source of only EoS.[36] On the specialisation of capital, some writers make it a source of both IRTS and EoS either unconditionally or with the qualification of fixed input prices.[37] Others list EoS only.[38]

Closely related to the ability to use more specialised capital as the scale of output expands is the ability to use different and better organisations of production, indeed both often occur at as one integrated set of changes. Two of our surveyed authors mention this, one as a source of EoS (Sloman 2006: 132) and the other as a source of both (Pass et al. 2005: 156, 475).

2.5 Once-for-all Costs

All of the sources cited so far affect the position and slope of the LRAC curve and so influence the firm's long-run decision on

---

[35] They state, 'Where economies of scale are present, a doubling of factor inputs results in a more than proportionate increase in output' (Pass et al. 2005: 475). They may of course be using the term EoS to mean IRTS.

[36] Pass et al. (2005: 156, 475), McConnell et al. (2012: 154) and Seldon and Penance (1976: 295) say IRTS and EoS, in McConnell's case given fixed input prices. Bain (1968: 492), Calhoun (2002: 137) and Pearce (1992: 122) say EoS only.

[37] These are Setterfield (2001: 489) Seldon and Pennance (1976: 120, 295) and Griffiths and Wall (2000: 171) unconditionally and Case et al. (2012: 196), Parkin et al. (2005: 214) and Perloff (2012: 172) with constant input prices.

[38] These are Abraham-Frois (2008: 232), Bain (1968: 492), Bannock et al. (2003: 114), Farrell (1997: 432), McAffee (2006: 4–101), Shim and Siegal (1995: 118) and Ammer and Ammer (1984: 415). Sloman (2006: 132) cites plant specialisation as a source of EoS without mentioning specialisation of capital equipment, although possibly it is meant to be included in plant specialisation.

the size of plant: major scale effects in plant and equipment make the SRATC curve steep while small effects make it flattish. We now come to a set of sources that do not affect the firm's long-run decision but do confer something similar to scale effects but only over the short run – a distinction made by none of those in our survey who discussed once-for-all costs.

One characteristic generic source in this group is a once-for-all fixed cost attached to the firm's entry into the relevant market for its product, other than those for plant and equipment. More detailed sources of this sort include the cost of acquiring a patent and other rights, legal costs, training costs and a host of other once-for-all startup costs.

These once-for-all fixed costs affect the size of the firm's profits but, being independent of the scale of output, they do not affect the size at which the firm will choose to enter.[39] Thus unlike the scale effects considered so far, these do not influence the selection of the firm's initial scale of operations and if conditions are static, will not influence any subsequent behaviour. However, if demand rises unexpectedly after the firm's size has been determined, there will be a short-term effect when these costs are spread over more units of output as the firm moves down its short-run cost average total curve. The firm is now inside its LRAC and in the long run will want to move to a new point on that curve as result of the increased demand – a point that once again is unrelated to the bygone cost of entry.

---

[39] Since many readers have doubted this result and its interesting implications, I give a simple proof for the case of a quadratic LRAC curve and a linear demand curve. Let the equation of the Viner envelope be $AVC = F/q - aq + bq^2$. Note that this not a production function but the equation of the U-shaped envelope, which tells the firm what combinations of output and unit costs it can chose when it enters. Let the demand be: $p = c - dq$. Totals are $TC = (AVC)q = F - aq^2 + bq^3$ and $TR = pq = cq - dq^2$. Total profit is: $TR - TC = \pi = cq - dq^2 - F + aq^2 - bq^3$. To choose the maximising location, differentiate π with respect to q and set the result equal to zero: $d\pi/dq = c - 2dq + 2aq - 3bq^2 = c - 2q(d-a) - 3bq^2 = 0$, which is a quadratic indicating the qs that maximises and minimises profits. Since it is independent of F, the entry value of q does not change, although the firm's profit does fall, as F increases. Note that this does not tell us anything about the firm's short run costs except that the equilibrium long run choice of q must also be on the relevant SRATC curve.

2.6   Mixed Cases

Many of the examples of these once-for-all costs that are cited in the literature are actually mixed cases that include both influences that affect the firm's long-run decision and those that do not do so, but do confer falling unit costs in the short run as just discussed.

A typical example of such a source is advertising costs. To be able to classify this alleged source of scale effects, we need some empirical knowledge – none of which was cited by the authors in our survey. At one extreme, a new firm entering with a new differentiated product may require some minimum amount of advertising to establish its market. This is similar to the cases just considered where once-for-all fixed costs do not affect the specifics of the entry decision (as long as they are not so high as to preclude profitable entry). Whether, after this minimum necessary amount of advertising the marginal returns to further advertising first rise then fall in a U-shaped fashion, or fall from the outset, is a matter that may well vary with time, place and type of commodity. On the assumption that sales vary directly with a given continuing flow of advertising expenditure, the additional advertising cost can be added to the marginal cost of production. The effect of these costs depends on the strength of the relation between advertising and sales. Depending on this elasticity, its contribution to marginal costs could be rising, falling or constant per unit of extra output. Unlike the case of the once-for-all fixed costs, these costs shift the firm's cost curves in various ways depending on the relations just discussed and so will shift the LRAC curve, but also in ways that cannot be determined until the relevant elasticities are known. But one way or the other, they do contribute scale effects that influence the firm's long-run decision concerning its scale of operations.

A similar case is provided by the R&D costs of developing a product that a new firm requires to enter the market. In the simplest case the detailed nature of the product, and hence sales, are independent of the cost of development – the product is either acceptable or it is not. In a more realistic case, the more that is spent on development, the better is the product and hence the greater the sales. In the first case, we have a simple fixed cost situation as already discussed. In the second case, everything depends, as with advertising, on the strength of the relation between R&D and sales. Depending on this elasticity there could be EoS, CoS or DoS to the expenditure on R&D. Of course, this is only a ceteris paribus scale effect. What happens to the firm's overall unit cost as output varies will depend on the sum of everything that affects this cost at the margin.

A related effect concerns the modern situation in which many firms must innovate a continual stream of new products in order to stay competitive. Such cases are taken up in section 3.

The Literature

Several authors in our survey refer to up-front costs as sources of scale effects, although none of them give a hint of any of the complications of which the above are just examples. These costs give rise to EoS according to some.[40] One author says they are a source of both EoS and IRTS without reservation,[41] while yet others say they are a source of both under the assumption of fixed input prices.[42] Advertising is cited by various authors as a source of either EoS or IRTS of both under the assumption of given input prices and others without such a qualification.[43]

2.7 Purely Pecuniary Sources

Although not always clear, the following cited sources may be pecuniary but in some circumstances may be based on real resource savings.

---

[40] These are Frank and Bernake (2009: 239), Bannock et al. (1984: 141, 2003: 114) and Barbosa-Filho (2008: 606).

[41] Krugman and Wells (2009: 323).

[42] These are Rutherford (2000: 142) and McConnell et al. (2012: 156).

[43] These are Brush (1994: 340) who refers more generally to marketing costs, Calhoun (2002: 137) who lists these as sources of DoS, and McConnell et al. (2012: 154–6), Pass et al. (2005: 156) and Seldon and Pennance (1976: 295) all of whom list them as a source of both EoS and IRTS – McConnell et al. with the qualification of fixed input prices, and Pass et al. and Seldon and Pennance unqualified.

Ammer and Ammer (1984: 415) refer to discounts on inputs in general and, separately, to 'greater bargaining power with labour unions banks and other lenders'. Access to, and favourable terms of obtaining, financial capital are cited by several who say they are sources of EoS, and two who say EoS and IRTS.[44] In so far as transportation costs vary in direct proportion to the amount shipped, these are not scale effects. In so far as quantity discounts become available as quantity shipped rises, they are pecuniary EoS to the firm whose goods are being shipped but may be real economies to the shipper if larger quantities require few resources per unit shipped than do smaller quantities.[45]

2.8   External Scale Effects

So far, we have dealt with cases where the scale effects are internal to the firm, either the producer of a final good or the producer of a capital good. We now consider some cases of sources that are mainly or wholly beyond the control the individual firm.

2.8.1   Network Effects

These can be defined in different ways. For one example, consider the output of a monopoly firm that is in the business of providing phone services to customers. Assume that each customer can be connected to the exchange at a constant cost and that the value of the phone service to the nth customer added is an increasing function of the number of other subscribers to whom she can connect. This firm can produce its connections at CRTS but can sell them at a price that is an increasing function of its size measured by the number of the customers that it serves. This is certainly a scale effect but not one that is covered by the conventional definitions of IRTS or

[44] EoS: Ammer and Ammer (1984: 415), Bain (1968: 492), Calhoun (2002: 137), Farrell (1997: 433), Pearce (1992: 122), Rutherford (2000: 142), Sloman (2006: 133), Abraham-Frois (2008: 232), and Bannock et al. (2003: 114). EoS and IRTS: Pass et al. (2005: 156) and Seldon and Penance (1976: 295).

[45] These are cited by Bain (1968: 492), Bannock et al. (2003: 114) and Case et al. (2012: 196) as sources of EoS.

EoS as it raises the value of output and hence the price at which it can be sold. Also as this example shows, it is not necessarily an external economy. It is certainly internal to the industry and, if the number of firms is small (one in the limit), it will be partially (or wholly in the limit) internal to the firm. The source of these scale effects is in the combinatorial nature of interconnections while the ability to exploit such latent effects depends on the size of the market. (For example, if a given percentage of the residents in some area want a service subject to a network effect, its per-customer value will increase as the total population increases.)

Network effects stemming from the demand rather than the cost side are listed by Frank and Bernake (2009: 238) as sources of EoS, while Krugman and Wells (2009: 323) say that they are sources of both IRTS and EoS.

2.8.2   Specialised Suppliers/Services

If the expansion of an assembly firm causes its suppliers to increase their outputs and thereby reach a lower point on their declining LRAC curves, there is an IRTD for the supplier firms and an EoS for the assembly firm.[46] In a rare case of complete agreement on whether we have a case of IRTS or EoS, these are listed as a source of EoS by all of the authors in our survey who mention them.[47]

2.8.3   Shared Infrastructure

There is little that can be concluded about any scale effects of shared infrastructure in the absence of much more information – except that in various circumstances it could generate no scale effects, an EOS or a DoS. To illustrate the possibilities, assume that the services of the infrastructure are an input to the firm in question and are provided at

---

[46] If one uses the type-2 meta-production function described in Section 1.4.5, this is a case of IRTS to the parts supplier. But viewed as either an IRTS or an IRTD, it is a real resource saving change from the view point of the pas supplier and an EoS from the assembler's.

[47] These are Ammer and Ammer (1984: 415), Farrell (1997: 434), Stockfisch (1968: 272), Sloman (2006: 133), Bannock et al. (2003: 114) Black et al. (2012: 123), Calhoun (2002: 137), Pearce (1992: 122) and Graaff (1987: 7599).

a constant price per unit of use, a price that might be zero (as with many roads) or some positive constant. Initially there is excess capacity on that facility. As all the firms in the industry expand, they get one of their 'inputs' at a constant price both before and after the expansion. Thus, there is no scale effect from their point of view. But the firm that is supplying the infrastructure encounters EoS as the fixed cost of creating the infrastructure is spread over more and more customers. If the infrastructure reaches capacity there will be an external DoS as the time and convenience costs of use to each firm rise as industry use rises. Now assume that the price that is charged for the use of the infrastructure's services is positively related to the unit cost of providing the service – a cost that is dominated by the high construction cost and hence a fixed cost to be spread over the users. Now each user will get an external EoS as industry use rises up to the facility's capacity. After that, as more and more users exacerbate the congestion, the internal time and convenience costs to the user will rise and eventually overcome any external gain from falling price due to more industry use. In another case, the provider of the infrastructure may impose a congestion charge that will impose an external DoS in addition to the internal costs imposed on each firm by the congestion. But as the congestion price rises, the congestion cost to users will fall if the price-disincentive is effective. On balance, the total cost to users may rise or fall depending on the elasticity of use with respect to the congestion charge. Hence there may be a range of EoS, of DoS and of CoS as overall use and eventually the congestion charge rise. Shared infrastructure without any further analysis is cited as a source of EoS by several of our authors.[48]

2.8.4 A Local Talent Pool?

Several writers list the development of a local talent pool as conferring an EoS.[49] It is difficult to determine that this is a source of EoS until one knows whose actions developed it and at what cost.

---

[48] These are Sloman (2006: 133), Abraham-Frois (2008: 232) and Graaff (1987: 7599).

[49] These are Farrell (1997: 434), Graaff (1987: 7599), Griffiths and Wall (2000: 173), Rutherford (2000: 142), Sloman (2006: 133) and Stockfisch (1968: 272).

2.9 Other Miscellaneous Causes

For completeness we give the few remaining causes that are mentioned by at least one of the authors that we have surveyed.

2.9.1 By-Products

Sloman (2006: 132) and Ammer and Ammer (1984: 415) cite the production of by-products as a source of scale economies. Although they do not specifically link this to indivisibilities, which they list separately, if there is a minimum size of operation for the production of any by-product, *ex ante* indivisibility, then as the firm's main activity is increased, it will at some point become profitable to produce by-products rather than treating their materials as wastes. The authors list this as a source of EoS for the firm.

2.9.2 Tax Relief?

It is difficult in the absence of much more information to see how tax relief confers an external scale effect. It is, however, cited by Abraham-Frois (2008: 232) as a source of EoS.

2.9.3 Learning by Doing?

A few authors cite learning by doing as a source of both EoS and IRTS, given fixed input prices.[50] It is hard to see this as a genuine scale economy. Rather it seems to be best regarded as a lag in the adjustment of costs to changes in output. If the scale of output is increased and new divisions of labour, new more specialised capital or new production processes are introduced, there will be a lag before labour has learned how to use the new processes with their full potential efficiency, a lag documented in many cases by

---

[50] Specifically, McConnell, et al. (2012: 156), Barbosa-Filho (2008: 606) and Setterfield (2001: 489). The last is the only one to provide a reason, which he states as follows: 'Experience can be accumulated simply by repeating a task at the same level of throughput. However, an increase in the number of "doers" . . . would also increase the stock of experience within a firm and may thus be associated with a more than proportional expansion of output' (489). There is no apparent reason for this assertion. Most learning-by-doing is associated with learning how to work efficiently with new technologies.

empirical learning curves. But if costs per unit of output fall at this higher scale of production, it is not due to learning by doing but by the increased productivity inherent in the new processes, while the time taken to learn how to master them is a lag but not a scale effect.

3 Constant and Variable Returns with Replication

We saw in Section 1.6.3 that where replication is possible, a firm's costs can be constant but only for integer multiples of the MES of the plant that defines the minimum point of the long-run envelope cost curve. Between those integer multiples the firm typically first encounters a range of DoS followed by a range of EoS.

3.1 *Replication with Non-Plant Specific Costs*

We also saw in that section that where the firm has significant costs that do not vary with the number of plants, it will encounter EoS over what can be an indefinitely large number of plants and hence firm size. (Here we confine ourselves to integer multiples of output of the optimum-sized plant.)

In many cases closely related to growth, the R&D costs of developing new products are large relative to the cost of manufacturing them. Consider a new product, say some new drug. Its high R&D costs were X and the MES for *production* of the new drug in each of its plants is at output q_1 and unit production cost c_1. Let the demand be such that n plants are fully employed in manufacturing the product. Now the unit cost for each plant, including its share of R&D costs, will be $c_1 + X/nq_1$, which is declining in n. For many firms these are not just once-for-all entry costs. Instead, a steady flow of new products is needed to maintain profits. In some, such as aircraft, if new products are not developed, the firm will find its sales falling, eventually to zero. In others, such as pharmaceuticals, the sale of new products during the lifetime of their patents is key to maintaining high profits. Since once patents expire, competition from generic forms of the product typically reduce profits greatly, a continual flow of new products is needed to maintain high profits. In these cases where R&D costs are large relative to production costs, average total costs fall dramatically as output and sales rise.

This type of effect also covers many retail industries. Modern fast food, garment retailers and motels are examples of the many industries that are replete with chains in which more or less identical 'plants' are operated, sometimes by the main firm and sometimes by independent franchisers, but all of whom gain EoS effects from a variety of centralised operations. For example, until the mid-1950s, most fast-food outlets were independently owned and operated. Then came the chains, first McDonald's and then others such as Burger King, Wendy's and A&W. They offered standardised menus and quality, both of which were highly variable in the earlier days. This increased the customer appeal of their products. Also several costs such as brand name advertising, centralised purchases and menu selection guided by consumer research, offered EoS that extended to an indefinitely large number of branches. Analogous comments apply to retailers such as Urban Outfitters and American Eagle, where centralised decisions regarding purchases, plant design and layout, sometimes in-house design of their product, and other related activities, confer EoS effects. Similar comments also apply to such hotel and motel chains as Holiday Inn, Marriot, Travelodge and Best Western.

In all of these cases, where replication of production facilities is possible, production at integer multiples of the MES of one plant will encounter an indefinite range of EoS. The size of all such firms is not limited by each reaching their MESs, but either by market demand if it is a monopolist or, more typically, by its ability to compete with other large firms operating similar but differentiated competing enterprises and all with unexploited EoS because of costs that can be spread over any number of plants.

Although several authors state that the US market is large enough for scale effects to be exhausted, this may be true of some industries, but is clearly not true for all the industries, including those mentioned above, in which non-plant specific costs are significant enough to confer an EoS on the firm as it increases the number of its 'plants' indefinitely. As noted, the size of such firms is not limited from the cost side but by competition from other firms with similar unlimited EoS.

3.2 Replication and the Constant-Returns Production Function

Many authors use the possibility of replicating plants, each producing at its MES, to imply the existence of a constant-returns PF for outputs larger than that produced by a single plant with costs such as $SRATC_5$ in Figure 1.[51] But this is not a valid implication. Let such a plant be producing at its cost-minimising point of y_1 and using input quantities x_1 and x_2. All that replication implies is that, where λ is an integer, the points $(\lambda x_1, \lambda x_2)$ in input space, all of which lie the ray through the origin of slope x_1/x_2, will be associated with outputs λy_1. To assume the existence of isoquants that pass through each of these points and are asymptotic to the axes, as is implied by a constant-returns PF, is to make the wholly unjustified assumption that the output y_1 that each duplicated plant would produce at its minimum-cost point can also be produced with technical efficiency by an array of different techniques that use the factors in all possible proportions. In other words, constant returns to one particular factor combination does not imply constant returns to other combinations, although it does imply a 'scalloped' long-run average cost curve with the same minimum point at the output that is an integer multiple of the outputs of the most efficient plant, as shown in Figure 2.

For example, it is unlikely that any fast-food outlet could operate effectively, if at all, at either extreme of almost all labour and little capital or (at least today) of almost all capital and almost no labour.

4 Sources of DoS

Unit costs can rise with the scale of output for reasons located both within the firm and at a higher level of aggregation. Causes within

---

[51] For example, Black et al. (2012: 111), Case et al. (2012: 199), Eatwell (2008: 140) and Varian (1992: 15).

the firm are related to individual pieces of capital equipment designed to do some job, the whole plant and the firm's organisation. Causes external to the firm occur at a more aggregated level and include such things as the costs of congestion and pollution. All of these can be sources of DoS and DRTD.

4.1 Internal Effects

4.1.1 Capital Equipment

There are many cases of diminishing returns to size in an individual piece of capital equipment due to physical laws. For example, if all the dimensions of a bridge are altered in the proportion λ, its structural strength is altered by $1/\lambda$ and its weight is altered by λ^3 (under the simplifying assumption that it is optimal to use the same types of materials in bridges of all sizes) (Adams 1991: 81). In other words, bridges and other similar structures, exhibit diminishing returns to design in the sense that as their size and the amount of materials used in their construction is increased, their strength decreases per unit of input. More generally, structural strength of any three-dimensional body tends to diminish as its dimensions are increased, *ceteris paribus*. Thus, a small-scale model can carry a heavier load expressed as a proportion of its size and weight, than can the scaled-up version. Also, a small model airplane can tolerate a hard landing that would destroy a larger version that had been scaled up proportionately. In many cases, resistance to turbulence arising from the motion of a body through a gas or a liquid increases more than in proportion to the increase in the dimensions of the body. As already discussed, many characteristics of ships exhibit increasing returns to size, but the fact that handling characteristics become increasingly sluggish as size is increased beyond some critical value is one of the factors that limit the economies of size that can be exploited.

As discussed earlier in this Element, many kinds of capital equipment are made of components that work together. Although one component may encounter increasing returns, if another cooperating component has decreasing returns, the whole typically has a range of IRTD followed by a range of DRTD. The smallest workable size is seldom the most efficient size. As size increases, most characteristics encounter favourable scale effects over some range. However, sooner or later many characteristics encounter decreasing returns which eventually dominate so that further increases in capacity now result in rising costs per unit of capacity delivered. The optimal size of a specific capital good is then the one at which the economies of scale in some aspects of the technology just balance the diseconomies in other aspects. The case of providing a flow of air to smelting ore discussed in more detail in Section 5 is a case in point. If we consider the whole history of this relation, we see unit costs falling over time as better and better technologies for injecting air into furnaces are developed. But the example also illustrates how increasing returns and decreasing returns to various parts of one composite technology can combine to produce U-shaped LRAC curves at any one time as the existing technology of providing air to the smelting ore limits the economic size of the smelter. Also as shown earlier in Carlaw (2004) and Carlaw and Lipsey (2008b: 223), the variable durability of the individual components of a specific capital good, combined with uncertainty, can lead first to a range of what we call IRTD followed by a range of DRTD, but which these writers call IRTS and DRTS.

These relations apply to many situations and are some of the most important sources of diminishing returns to design that limit the extent to which other sources of increasing returns can be exploited by building larger versions of some generic capital good – once again both geometrical properties and physical laws contribute to these relations.

4.1.2   The Plant

Similarly, to individual capital goods, individual production facilities typically have an efficient size beyond which cost per unit of output begins to increase. This is partly determined by the scale effects of the individual pieces of capital equipment that are incorporated into the plant as well as by more macro characteristics of the plant itself. For example, there is an upper limit to the speed at which any production facility can be operated efficiently. There are many factors that determine the most efficient speed, such as the frictions created as machinery, including robots, are speeded up. But that there is an upper limit can be easily seen by the *reductio ad absurdum* argument that if an assembly line operated at the speed of sound an intolerable sonic boom would be created.

4.1.3 The Firm

In the literature on scale effects, it is commonly argued that because of the possibility of replication, one should never expect to see diminishing returns to scale at the firm level. We have already considered increasing costs in the interval between integer multiples of the most efficient plant. Here we consider variations in unit costs at integer multiples of the output of the most efficient sized plant.

Writing in the *New Palgrave*, Eatwell argues without recourse to empirical evidence that 'barring indivisibilities, there can be no barrier to replication ... In other words, there can be no such things as decreasing returns *to scale*' (2008: 166, Italics in the original). In a similar vein Silvestre (1987: 2897) states 'an exact clone of the production process that exhaustively lists all factors of production should give exactly the same output. The failure to double the output suggests the presence of an extra input, not listed among the arguments of the PF that cannot be duplicated.' This replication argument against decreasing returns to a firm is also used by Black et al. (2012: 111) and Frank (2008: 280–1) who repeat the argument that DRTS are a result of unspecified inputs being held constant as production is increased so that there are no genuine DRTS. Similarly, Varian (1992: 16) holds that DRTS due a fixed input is 'the most natural case' of DRTS – although he does not go on to consider any 'less natural cases'. Finally, Cowell (2006: 126) rules out DRTS after defining them away with an axiom of additivity that applies unless 'certain essential features of the firm are non-expandable'. This last qualification might cover some of the considerations given below, although it is not precise enough to allow us to be sure what the author had in mind.

These arguments against decreasing returns to scale assume that replication is always possible in any relevant production process, as long as there are neither input indivisibilities nor hidden non-variable inputs. The qualifications just listed raise the empirical question: 'Under what specific circumstances is replication possible?' But this is an issue that cannot be settled by a *priori* reasoning alone. Of course, if the list of possible inputs is defined as *anything* that might cause the PF to display decreasing returns without detailed specification of these exceptions, the proposition becomes tautological and hence uninteresting empirically. As is well known, propositions about real behaviour cannot be deduced from definitional identities.

To go further requires an appeal to empirical evidence. Here we can only illustrate some of the empirical possibilities. On the one hand, to produce more razor blades, a new plant identical to existing ones can be set up in a green field and managed independently. This should yield CRTS and CoS for integer multiples of the output of the most efficient plant's MES. On the other hand, if more output is required at a point in space, or less stringently, if spatial location matters in any significant way, it may be impossible to replicate exactly. For example, Eaton and Lipsey have argued in number of publications (see e.g. Eaton &Lipsey 1977, 1997) that when space is introduced into the neoclassical model, many new considerations become important and many common generalisations no longer hold. Lipsey, Carlaw and Bekar (2005: 400) give another example, this one concerning the draining of early coal mines where it was necessary to deliver power at the pit head to operate pumps. Until the steam engine was invented, pumps were operated by horses turning capstans and although there is no limit to the amount of energy that can be obtained from horses if there is room for them to operate, there were physical limits to the number that could be applied to any one pithead. Also, long before that absolute limit was reached, costs per horsepower increased due to such problems as non-linear increases in difficulties of coordinating the operation of horses, both when at work and when changing shifts.

As is true in so much of the economics literature concerning the firm, the replication argument applies most commonly to manufacturing firms. However, these constitute a relatively small and declining portion of GDP in most advanced economies. In contrast, firms in the primary producing sectors cannot easily replicate. Those in mining and forestry find each production location unique in many relevant characteristics and, although possibly less so, this is also important with farmers. Similar considerations apply to retailers. Every location in a city is unique and although some are more or less similar to some others, it is rarely possible to duplicate exactly all of the relevant characteristics of two different locations. Also, many high tech firms find that the externalities associated with clustering of related firms are important in determining costs so that costs rise with distance from the centre of the cluster.

Thus, replication is possible in some circumstances, where no worse than constant returns is predicted for integer multiples of the smallest plant that has the lowest minimum-cost point, and not in others where the DRTS may apply. Where replication is possible is an empirical matter that cannot be settled by *a priori* reasoning.

Carlaw and Lipsey (2008b: 223) are alone among the authors surveyed in referring to inputs that are not reproducible due to spatial relations as a source of DoS. Mansfield (1979) mentions increasing geographical size of a market as scale increases, presumably leading to increased costs of both delivered inputs and outputs.

Two other alleged sources of DoS for firms are frequently mentioned in the literature but might work in either direction of increasing or diminishing unit costs as scale rises. The first is organisational complexity (managerial complexity, bureaucratic complexity). In the absence of compelling empirical evidence, there seems no reason in today's world of automated and robotised production to assume a systematic positive relation between scale and the complexity of organisation, nor a negative one between the latter and unit costs. Neither, of course, is there any strong reason to deny that they might be causes of non-negative scale effects under circumstances that remain to be specified. In the literature surveyed, these complexities were listed as sources of DoS by many authors.[52] Others list them as causes of DRTS.[53] Some list them as both DoS and DRTS without qualification,[54] while list them as both with the qualification that input prices be constant.[55]

The second commonly alleged source is labour conflict (worker motivation, etc.). Once again, in the absence of compelling evidence there seems no reason in today's world of automated and robotised production to assume a systematic positive relation between scale and labour conflict. Small firms can have labour problems just as can medium and large firms. Nonetheless, various authors list them either as sources of DoS or DRTS.[56]

Finally, one author, Rutherford, mentions materials fatigue as a source of both DoS and DRTS, providing that input prices are fixed, although there is no apparent reason for assuming that materials are more prone to fatigue the larger the scale of production

4.2   External Effects

The first two sources listed here are genuine scale effects not already discussed.

4.2.1   Increasing Factor Prices

The classic case in economic theory is the Hecksher-Ohlin two-industry GE model where both industries have constant-returns PFs that use the two factors in different proportions. Factor prices

---

[52]   These are Ammer and Ammer (1984: 415), Bain (1968: 492), Brush (1994: 339), Farrell (1997: 433), Jackson (1996: 230), Mankiw (2006: 274), Sloman (2006: 133), Bannock et al. (2003: 100), Abraham-Frois (2008: 232), Black et al. (2012: 111, 123), Rutherford (2000: 123), McAffee (2006: 4–101) and Shim and Siegal (1995: 106).

[53]   These are Case et al. (2012: 200), Perloff (2012: 172), Pindyck and Rubinfeld (2009: 215) and Mansfield (1979: 143).

[54]   These are Krugman and Wells (2009: 323), Seldon and Penance (1976: 120, 295) and Pass et al. (2005: 134).

[55]   These are McConnell et al. (2012: 156) and Parkin et al. (2005: 215).

[56]   Black et al. (2012: 111, 123), Brush (1994: 339) and McAffee (2006: 4–101) list these as sources of DoS, while Case et al. (2012: 200) and Perloff (2012: 172) say they are sources of DRTS, while McConnell et al. (2012: 156) says they are sources of both with the qualification that input prices be constant.

change as one firm expands and the other contracts in a general equilibrium context for the whole economy, causing the cost of output to rise in one industry and fall in the other. Of course there will be less general cases as when the expansion of one industry increases its demand for an industry-specific input. These are obviously not DRTS as the source is not in the PF of the final goods producer. Instead they are pecuniary DoS effects. Such increasing prices may also result from a real diseconomy if firms supplying the inputs face rising real unit costs and hence must raise the price of the input they supply to a final goods producer.[57]

4.2.2   Congestion and Pollution

These are typically external to the firm and often to the industry. But they can be internal to either as when a single firm in a company town increases its output causing increased pollution that has a non-linear effect on its real costs. When pollution alters the firm's PF by causing the same inputs to produce less output, we have a case that is not strictly any of DRTS, DoS or DRTD. If congestion raises a firm's real delivery costs, and if we define output to include delivery to markets, we get DRTS even with replication as the one cost rises more than in proportion to all the others. Or this may be a case of DoS as when congestion raises the prices of the firm's inputs. The majority of our authors who cited one or both of these as sources classify them as causing DoS, while some others select either DRTS or both.[58]

4.2.3   Other Listed Sources

A few other minor alleged sources are listed by the authors in our sample. Transportation distances are mentioned by Bannock et al.

---

[57] These price effects are listed by Kamerschen and Valentine (1977: 236), Bannock et al. (1984: 142), Sloman (2006: 134), McAffee (2006: 4–102) and Shim and Siegal (1995: 106) as sources of DoS.

[58] Abraham-Frois (2008: 232), Bannock et al. (2003: 100, 1984: 127), Stockfisch (1968: 269) and Bohm (2008: 189) list both of these as sources of DoS, while congestion alone is listed by Pass et al. (2005: 188) as a source of both DRTS and DoS, by Frevert (1997: 1376) as a source of DRTS and Farrell (1997: 434) as a source of DoS.

(2003: 114) who makes them a source of DoS. However, these are an example of the importance of geographical factors previously emphasised in our discussion of internal DRTS. The marginal cost of attracting new customers is listed by Rutherford (2000: 123) as a source of both DoS and DRTS, assuming that input prices are constant. This has already been discussed above in the section on advertising where we argue that it is internal to the firm and may be the cause of EoS or DoS. Finally, infrastructure deterioration is listed by Abraham-Frois (2008: 232) as a source of DoS. If infrastructure is maintained there is no issue here; if it is not, then it is hard to see this neglect as being positively associated with scale. This is typical of the ad hoc suggestions that are so often provided in many of the cases cited above that might go either way, or more likely, not be associated systematically with increases in output.

5   Conditions Leading to the Exploitation of Scale Effects

The main topic of this Element is the sources of scale effects. However, the discussion of this issue suggests some obvious points on the conditions favouring the exploitation of such effects, which we now mention with no pretence of giving an exhaustive survey of the issue.

5.1   Market Size

Ever since Adam Smith; discussion of specialisation in the pin factory, it has been accepted that size of market is an important determinant of how many of the latent scale economies are actually exploited. This was also the thrust of Allyn Young's essay already mentioned. Although he did not use this distinction, both indivisibilities and design effects are important in this context. As long as capital goods and specialised processes have an *ex ante* indivisibility, scale effects associated with them will not be exploited if market demand is not high enough to employ these production facilities at their minimum indivisible size. Further scale economies associated with design economies (covering the range from SRATC$_1$ to SRATC$_5$ in Figure 1) will only be exploited when demand is sufficient to purchase the resulting output. Such expansions of demand may be associated with the rise of some particular industry or with general economic growth that increases the demand for all products with positive income elasticities.

5.2   Historical Increasing Returns

Lipsey, Carlaw and Bekar (2005) stress the ubiquity of latent scale effects in our world and observe that the ability to exploit these at any one point in time is limited by existing technologies. Then as new technologies are developed, such scale effects can be further exploited leading to temporary, but often prolonged, periods of increasing returns while this is being done. Since these are disequilibrium effects, they will not be captured by static models in which all transitory effects have been eliminated.

One of the examples they cite concerns the smelting of ore where the heat loss is proportional to the surface area of the ore's receptacle while the service rendered is proportional to its cubic capacity, thus creating a scale economy in size. But to work efficiently, air must be infused into the whole body of ore being smelted. The ability to exploit the physical economies arising from the relation between surface area and volume was limited through historical time by the ability to deliver the needed air as the size of the receptacle was increased. For any given technology of delivering this air, it becomes harder and harder to deliver an even flow of air to all parts of the receptacle as its size was increased, yielding eventually decreasing returns to the size of any smelting process using a given air-injection method. Early ore was smelted in open fires and such smelting was efficient at only a very small scale. Later it was placed in a kiln and hand operated bellows delivered the needed air. When blast furnaces replaced kilns, water-wheel-operated, and later yet, steam-engine-operated, bellows greatly increased the efficient size of smelters. Then pressurising, and also preheating the air to be injected, increased the efficient size even further so that more of the ubiquitous scale economies related to surface area and volume could be exploited.

There are many other important cases of such historical increasing returns. They depend critically on the exploitation of scale effects that already exist in nature but cannot currently be exploited because of limitations in complementary technologies. For another example, larger passenger aircraft tend to have lower material inputs in construction and lower costs in operation per passenger mile than smaller aircraft. But the ability to build larger aircraft has evolved over time as the technologies of both design and materials have been steadily improved.

5.3   Policy Changes

In the above cases new innovations were required to exploit the scale economies. Cases where growth of markets provided the opportunity for the exploitation of scale effects without the need for the invention of new technologies are clearest where barriers to trade have been reduced through public policy. Before the European Common Market was formed economists using the then standard trade theory in which each country produced an array of well-defined homogeneous products had predicted that various countries would specialise in different products – e.g., one in cars, one in furniture, one in TVs, etc. Because the full significance of product differentiation has not been appreciated, the outcome was quite different than expected. Different countries specialised in different versions of each generic commodity. Scale economies were exploited as countries reduced the number of versions of each generic commodity that it produced, increasing the volume of output in the versions in which it specialised and reaping associated scale economies. Similar effects were observed when Canada and the United States formed a free trade area. These gains from scale economies were of course additional to the gains from the reallocation of resources according to local comparative advantage.

The sources of these scale effects can be studied in static treatments of economies that exist *either exploited or unexploited* at any one time. There is nothing in this static approach that is inconsistent with Lipsey, Carlaw and Bekar's (2005) studies of evolving economies. In most of this Element we have followed the majority or writers in concentrating on the *sources* of scale effects while accepting that two of the forces that allow these effects to be *exploited over time* are the growth of the economy and the development of new technologies. All we are doing is distinguishing between the sources of scale effects that exist independently of time, as studied by the literature on scale effects, and the conditions that allow their exploitation to alter over time, as studied in economic history and economic theory.

5.4   Which Came First: New Technologies or Growth in Market Growth?

Growth in market size and new scale-exploiting technologies interact in a system of positive feedback, although it is possible to argue sometimes that one was at least the proximate cause of the other. We first consider two important historical cases where a general increase in market size was an important cause of growth in the now-advanced countries. But each of these expansions in market size were themselves caused by a technological advance that was not itself primarily a response to general economic growth. The first was the great expansion of European trade that followed the development of the three-masted sailing ship and the subsequent spread of European trade over much of the world (as discussed, for example, by Mokyr (1990)). The three-masted sailing ship, with square sails on the two forward masts, a lateen sail on the after mast and triangular sails on an extended bowsprit, evolved as the Portuguese slowly felt their way down the coast of Africa looking for a sea route to India. It was not previous economic growth that motivated these explorations but, among other things, the difficulties associated with European access to the land route to the East. Once fully developed, this new type of ship allowed merchants to sail the world over in search of valuable cargoes with a reasonable chance of returning home. This initiated a bout of what Mokyr calls Smithian growth – economic growth that results from a rapid growth in trade. As it developed through the sixteenth century, it exploited many scale economies in transportation, distribution and administration, going on to become an early example of truly globalised trade.

The second case concerns the development of American trans-continental railways, which fused many local markets into one large national market. The railroad was the natural application of the steam engine. The high pressure engine developed at the beginning of the nineteenth century had applications for non-stationary power delivery which were apparent to those concerned with both land and sea transport. The railway lowered transport costs while raising the reliability and speed of overland transportation. These developments were particularly important in the vast expanses of North America compared with the relatively small size of the United Kingdom where the engine was first developed. By welding the US market into a single whole for many products, it lead to the exploitation of an array of scale economies and regional specialisations according to comparative advantage, both of which raised productivity and output, leading to economic growth (see Chandler 1990: 53–8).

Some more general evidence suggests that developments in technology not directly induced by economic growth were also the proximate cause in many other cases. This comes from the relative growth rates of technologies that have driven growth and those that are being more or less dragged along by it. Although overall economic growth is responsible for the steady rise in market size measured in real purchasing power units, most of the increases in the markets associated with many of the new technologies that at one time or another were leaders in growth, such as the various electronic devices that have been developed in Silicon Valley and other similar agglomerations of innovative talent, have been high *relative to* the general growth in market size of the economies in which they have occurred. In such cases, overall economic growth seems to be more a consequence of the arrival of these new technologies and the new markets that they often created, rather than these new technologies being enabled by a growth in the overall size of the national market.

A case where growth was arguably the proximate cause of technological development that then contributed to further growth is the steam engine. As Britain's economic growth proceeded in the seventeenth and eighteenth centuries, the demand for coal increased and coal mines went deeper underground where flooding became increasingly important. The demand for removing water led to a series of inventions that culminated in Newcomen's atmospheric engine early in the eighteenth century. This was a clear case of general growth providing the incentive for technological advance. But the incentives for the subsequent turning of the atmospheric engine into a genuine steam-driven engine undertaken by James Watt is not so clear. Once developed the steam engine's use spread through the economy in the late eighteenth and early nineteenth centuries, contributing to economic growth particularly when combined with new innovations in textile production.

Although much can be said about these historical events and many others that are similar to them, this is not an Element on economic history. There are two conceptually distinct sequences. In one, economic growth influences the growth of markets, which in turn influences the technological change that underlies shifts in firms' long-run cost curves when firms exploit scale effects. In the other technological changes allow the exploitation of scale economies that contribute to bursts of rapid growth. There is little doubt that both of these interact in positive feedback loops and that the new technologies, whether they were the cause or the consequence of economic growth, often succeed in exploiting untapped scale economies.

6 Consequences of Exploiting Scale Effects

There is an extensive literature on the consequences of scale effects, which is beyond the scope of this Element. Here we only mention one or two key points, again with no pretence of giving an exhaustive survey of the issue.

Many of the early writers on development economics emphasised the importance of scale effects that could be exploited when economic development got underway. In his masterly essay 'The Rise and Fall of Development Economics', Paul Krugman notes the importance given to scale effects by writers in the tradition of Albert Hirschman (1958). He argues that because they could not, or would not, model economies subject to these scale effects, their writings fell into obscurity, ignored by economists whose models almost exclusively assumed constant returns. He goes on to show how Murphy et al. (1989) restored interest in this approach by modelling in ways relevant to development economics, economies subject to scale effects.

Another writer whose important works on the effects of scale effects were ignored for years while constant returns was the order of the day's modelling was Brian Arthur, many of whose writings on this issue are reprinted in a collection of essays (Arthur 1994).

In his seminal article incorporating endogenous technological change into a macro growth model, Paul Romer (1990) assumed universal scale economies associated with all such changes, a phenomenon that subsequent researchers were unable to establish conclusively using empirical evidence. Later, Carlaw and Lipsey (2011) separated scale effects and endogenous technological change by developing a growth model in which endogenously generated general-purpose technologies produced sustained growth without any non-constant scale effects. What has not been done as yet is to build a model of endogenous growth in which scale effects are present but constrained in the amount by which they can be exploited by the forces discussed in this Element.

7   Conclusion and Summary

In conclusion, we summarise some of our most important results.

The world in which we live, with its three dimensions, physical laws and random components of much of its behaviour, is replete with non-linear relations that give rise to scale effects. But exploitation of these scale effects is limited both by the extent of the market and by decreasing returns to some of the components of capital goods and production facilities such as the reduction in structural strength of many bodies as dimensions are increased proportionally. Thus, if we consider alternative sizes of a machine designed to do a particular job, or of a whole plant designed to produce a particular product, the unit costs of whatever is being produced will typically fall over a range of outputs starting from zero up at to some critical value, after which it will begin to rise – in other words the long-run average total cost curve for the production of a product by a plant (or machine) will be U-shaped. For small changes in the scale of output, firms may use a larger version of what is basically the same production process, but for large changes wholly new production techniques will be adopted, requiring different kinds of equipment and a differently trained labour force, things that are difficult, if not impossible, to capture within the confines of a single production function. The falling unit costs associated with these effects are called economies of design in this Element.

Also, the operation of multiplying all physical inputs by some constant has few real-world counterparts. For this reason, we replace the textbook definition of returns to scale with the concept of returns to design: what happens to costs when output is varied over the long run using the lowest available cost of producing each output.

Although indivisibilities are commonly cited in the literature as a major source of scale effects, the various meanings that can be, and commonly are, given to the term are not typically distinguished. All capital goods with differentiated parts are *ex post* indivisible in the sense that parts of them will typically produce nothing. This universal characteristic of such capital goods cannot, therefore, be used to explain why firms encounter different scale effects at different scales of output, although some writers have assumed that they could.

Most, but not all capital goods, plants and individual pieces of equipment, have minimum sizes at which they are *ex ante* indivisible, no smaller size will do the job. *Ex ante* indivisibilities of plants cause unit costs to be negatively associated with output only when it is efficient to use the smallest plant that will produce the product. *Ex ante* indivisibilities of pieces of capital equipment contribute to a negative relation of unit costs and output only when the capital good cannot be made smaller even though the current level of production will not allow the smallest feasible version to be employed up to its full capacity. If individual pieces of capital only came in one size, the plant that uses them would have to operate the output that was the lowest common multiple of the capacities of its individual capital goods so as to achieve the lowest possible unit cost. But if capital goods can be made in various sizes down to some minimum possible size that will do its job, the plants cost's will fall as output rises for this reason until it reaches the output of the smallest possible version of the machine with the largest minimum capacity and other machines (whose *ex ante* indivisibility is at a lower capacity) will be designed to have the same capacity.

Some capital goods, such as pipelines, have no *ex ante* indivisibilities, being producible at any size needed to do any specific job. Thus, the design economies that they confer have nothing to do with any (non-existent) indivisibilities.

Each firm has the option of reconfiguring its production processes or duplicating the most efficient one for integer multiples of the output of its MES. Where exact duplication is possible, the firm should not have to accept diseconomies of scale for integer multiples of the outputs at their MES. But although microtheory takes place on the head of a pin, actual production takes place in space, and where spatial conditions matter, exact duplication is often not possible so that diseconomies may have to be accepted.

The firm that is duplicating production facilities may still encounter economies of scale, particularly when there are large costs that are specific to the firm but not to the individual plant and do not depend on the scale of output. The size of such firms is then not typically limited by cost considerations but by their ability to compete with similar firms each having a large number of more or less identical 'plants' (such as fast-food outlets, clothing stores and hotels).

The above sources of economies and diseconomies are real in the sense that they depend on variations in the amount of inputs needed per unit of output. However, it is virtually impossible to analyse them using a single PF defined as it usually is to relate physical inputs to output. If we wish to have inputs that are used at all scales of output, it is necessary to use indexes of a few broad classes of inputs. Even then, the PF will not fully span the resulting input space since many of its points will be technically inefficient – although they give the maximum output that can be produced by the indicated inputs, that output could be produced with a different input ratio that uses less of all inputs. For example, for very small outputs, craft methods are often technically efficient while it is technically inefficient to use complex machines whose *ex ante* indivisibilities occur at high levels of output, while for large scales of output craft methods that use much labour and simple forms of capital equipment are often technically inefficient.

The typical firm also encounters pecuniary economies of scale as the prices of its inputs change with its scale of operations. Some of these are the result of real upstream changes as design economies are reaped by firms operating at these earlier stages of production, as more efficient machines can be hired or as quantity discounts result from lower real costs of supplying inputs in bulk. Others are purely pecuniary as when the firm is able to force down the price of its inputs as a result of growing market power in input markets.

The exploitation of the above scale economies is both a cause and a consequence of growth in evolving economies. Three of the major changes that allow the vast range of latent scale economies to be exploited are (1) general economic growth that increases demand for products whose production encounters favourable scale effects; (2) the development of new technologies that remove limits that prevent existing technologies from further exploiting their latent scale effects; and (3) policy changes that enlarge market size. Sometimes the problems and opportunities associated with economic growth help to induce technological changes that then exploit favourable scale effects, while at other times the new technologies are developed for reasons unrelated to growth but then became causes of growth as they exploit latent scale effects.

It would appear that all of these things can be adequately studied using the traditional concepts of scale effects, once returns to scale are replaced by returns to design (thus avoiding the artificial exercise of multiplying all physical inputs by the same constant). Although these effects contribute to dynamic changes in the economy, comparative statics exercises analyzing how a firm's and an industry's physical inputs and its costs vary as its output undergoes a single once-for-all change can provide all that as needed for understanding how scale effects influence the ongoing growth of an economy. No novel new definition of scale effects involving continual dynamic changes seems to be needed.

Appendix A

Table of Definitions

Scale effects: Anything that affects the firm's real or money unit costs as a result of changing its scale of operations.

> *Real resource effect:* There is a change in the amount of inputs per unit of output.

> *Pecuniary effect:* There is a change in the price of one or more of the firm's inputs with no related reduction in real resources used per unit of output.

Efficiency effects: Variations in unit costs as production is varied over the long run. Also called efficiencies of scale.

> *EoS:* Unit costs fall as output is expanded over the long run.

> *DoS:* Unit costs rise as output is expanded over the long run.

> *CoS:* Unit costs remain constant as output is expanded over the long run.

Efficiencies of design: Variations in unit costs as production is varied over the long run due to the replacement of one PF-1 by another. Similar to 'efficiency effects' except that it refers explicitly to the replacement of one PF by another.

> *EoD:* The change in PF needed to accomplish an increase in the scale of output leads to a reduction in unit costs.

> *DoD:* The change in PF needed to accomplish an increase in the scale of output leads to an increase in unit costs.

> *CoD:* The change in PF needed to accomplish an increase in the scale of output leaves unit costs unchanged.

Returns effects: Variations in physical output resulting from variations in inputs over the long run. Also called returns to scale.

> *IRTS:* An equi-proportionate change in all inputs results in a more than proportionate change in the output.

CRTS: An equi-proportionate change in all inputs results in the same proportionate change in the output.

DRTS: An equi-proportionate change in all inputs results in a less than proportionate change in the output.

Replication of a capital good: Creating more units identical to those already in use.

Reconfiguration of a capital good: Using differently designed capital goods.

Type-1 production function (PF-1): Gives the maximum output that can be produced by each given bundle of inputs on the assumption that the firm is using a specific technology of production.

Type-2 production function (PF-2): Gives the maximum output that can be produced by each given bundle of inputs on the assumption that the firm can utilise any technology of production that is currently available.

Ex post *divisibility and indivisibility:* Refers to altering an individual capital good or plant once it has been produced.

Ex ante *divisibility and indivisibility:* Refers to altering the size of a capital good or whole plant, making a new one that is larger or smaller than the original one but that can do the same type of job.

ncrs-indivisibilities (for non-constant returns to scale indivisibilities): A production process is divisible in this sense if it can be scaled upward or downward by multiplying all of the inputs in its production function by some positive constant, λ, and have its output change in the same proportion. The process is defined to be indivisible in the downward direction if the result is to alter output by some multiple, γ, where $0 \leq \gamma < \lambda$.

mps-indivisibility (for minimum possible size): A plant is defined as *ex ante* mps-divisible if a smaller version can be made to do the same type of job as the larger version. The smallest size plant that can produce the product in question is *ex ante mps*-indivisible at that size.

Appendix B

Problems with Production Functions

There are several problems associated with either or both type-1 and type-2 production functions. To start we note some typical definitions of the PF drawn from the literature.

B1. Definitions

If all available inputs are used, at any time, then there will be a maximum attainable amount of product (output) that can be produced by each and every combination of inputs – that is, the maximum amount of product that can be attained from any specific combination of inputs that existing technology (know-how) permits – is called the production function.

Feiwel and Feiwel (1997: 1229)

The firm's production function $f(z_1, z_2)$ shows the maximum output which can be produced from the input combination (z_1, z_2)

Gravelle and Rees (1992: 180)

Given values for all the inputs and values for all but one output, the production function specifies the maximum attainable value for the remaining output.　　　　　　　Henderson (1994: 811)

The production function for a firm shows the maximum output which can be produced with specific levels of inputs, given the available technology.　　　　　　　McAuliffe (1999: 165)

The production function shows only the maximum amount of output that can be produced from given levels of labor and capital, *because the production function includes only efficient production processes.*　　　　　　Perloff (2012: 155, italics added)

In constructing this [production] function, all methods, techniques, or processes that require more of one input and no less of any other input are rejected.   Smith (1968: 512)

B2. Alternative Factor Combinations at a Given Output

Consider the typical textbook shape of a two-input PF's isoquant such as shown by I_1 in Figure 4. The highly capital-intensive techniques used at the left-hand end of this isoquant must be very different from the highly labour-intensive techniques used at the right-hand end of I_1. Students are not typically invited to think about such things, and, if they do, they probably conceive of a putty-style capital that can be spread evenly and more or less thickly over the labour force. To get closer to reality while still stylising, assume that there are four production techniques whose most efficient K/L ratios at some given relative price of the two inputs are given by the slopes of the lines E_1 for robotised, E_2 for mass produced, E_3 for artisan-style with a high degree of specialisation of labour using specialised tools and E_4 for artisan-style with a low degree of specialisation of labour using simple tools. If the level of output given by this isoquant is very large, it is highly unlikely that techniques 3 or 4 could produce efficiently at that scale, and possibly not even technique 2. Assume that this is so. Now the amounts of K and L needed to produce the output indicated by a_1 using each of the three non-robotised techniques are, for example, respectively, a_2, a_3 and a_4, all of which are technically inefficient for that output. So technique 1 will be used for that level of output whatever is the relative price of K and L.

Some readers have found it counter-intuitive that the best combination for techniques that use the ratios E_2 to E_4 could be technically inefficient at some output levels. To see the conditions for this let a_1 in Figure 4 represent an output of y_3 produced with inputs k_3 and l_3. Let the most efficient sized plant that uses the inputs in the ratio indicated by E_4 have the much smaller output output y_4 produced by inputs k_4 and l_4. Processes using the ratio

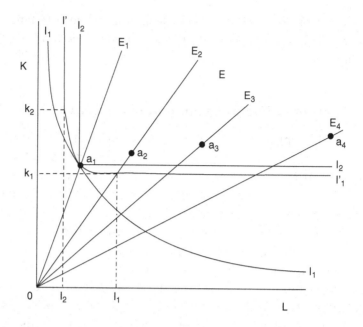

Figure 4 Factor inputs with four different production technologies

indicated by E_4 will be technically inefficient to the process using the ratio E_1 whenever $k_4/k_3, l_4/l_3 > y_4/y_3$. For example, if the output of the most efficient E_4-type plant is 10 per cent that of the output at a_1 while the capital and labour inputs are respectively 12 per cent and 20 per cent of those at a_1, the 10 duplicated E_4-type plants needed to produce the same output as a_1 will use respectively 120 per cent and 200 per cent of the capital and labour used at a_1.

We now see a problem with the common definitions of the PF that were illustrated above. If we insist on saying that it gives the maximum that can be produced from every possible combination of the specified inputs, as do most definitions of the PF, we must include points a_2, a_3 and a_4 and others like them. This makes the defined isoquant in the case illustrated positively sloped over most of its range. Or if we follow Smith, or the Italicised portion of Perloff's definition, the isoquant for the production associated with input combination a_1 spans only a small part of the input space, covering just the input combinations that can be produced efficiently by a robotised plant. Some substitution between labour and capital may be possible within that basic technology. But the scope for this will be small in any robotised plant as shown by the isoquant labelled I'_1. That line becomes horizontal not far to the right of a_1 (the point l_1, k_1) indicating that no further efficient substitutions of labour for capital are possible in robotised production, and vertical not far to the left of a_1 (the point l_2, k_2), indicating a minimum amount of labour that is needed for any existing robotised production technique. So without too much violence to the facts, we can assume that the ratio is fixed, giving a Leontief-style isoquant as shown by I_2. So the isoquant I_1 has degenerated to the point a_1, or if some substitution between K and L is possible in the robotised plant, the segment of curve I'_1 that lies between the points k_1, l_1 and k_2, l_2.

So, if we define the PF as indicating only technically efficient factor combinations, most of the factor space in this example will be empty: there is no technically efficient way in which to use the factor amounts indicated by these points. For high levels of outputs, most of the technically efficient points will lie close to E_1 because there is no technically efficient way to produce large outputs of many goods and services using a large amount of labour and a very few simple tools. Indeed, in many cases there will be no way to do it, even inefficiently, if the good's production requires some complex machines that cannot be dispensed with. For example, silicon chips could not be produced by simple craft forms of production using much labour and only simple tools. In contrast for low levels of output, the efficient points will lie close to E_3 and E_4 because there is no technically efficient way to produce a small output of most manufactured goods using only a small amount of labour and a large amount of complex capital goods, most of which would have to lie idle most of the time because they had reached the minimum size at which they became *mps*-indivisible. In the absence of detailed technical information, there is nothing to rule out the possibility of such blank spaces in most production functions.

Some theoretical treatments make formal assumptions that ensure that the isoquants are asymptotic to the axes. This implicitly assumes that the array of existing technologies is such that every possible ratio of inputs can be make technically efficient at every possible level of output. Of course, students are only asked to follow the formal treatment of such assumptions and seldom if ever asked to consider what impossible things these imply about behaviour in the real world.

B3. Expansion Paths at Given Factor Prices

Now consider Figure 5 where we assume that the K/L ratio is constant at all levels of output for each production process at the relative price shown by the slope of the equal outlay SS curves. Assume that for any location in factor space between the lines S_1 and S_2 the outputs associated with the actual or near-Leontief-style isoquants for the four processes that are 'tangent' to the price line stand in the order $x(E_1) > x(E_2) > x(E_3) > x(E_4)$. As total output is decreased, lowering the S line, it will reach a position where the 'tangent' indicates a higher isoquant for process 2 than 1, then for 3 over than 2 and finally 4 than for 3. As this occurs, each more capital-intensive production process will be abandoned for a less capital intensive one. Each time this happens, the K/L ratio will change abruptly to that indicated by the slope of E_2, then E_3 and finally E_4. The expansion path for this relative price will thus follow the heavy broken line starting from 0 and going through all the xs from x_1 to x_7.

B4. PFs with Replication and Resulting Constant Returns to Scale

Many treatments argue that a constant-returns PF, such as a Cobb-Douglas PF, can be used when firms are large enough to have more than one replicated production facility. Assume for illustration that the optimum-sized plant has an output associated with the inputs shown by x_6. All that replication assures is that the outputs

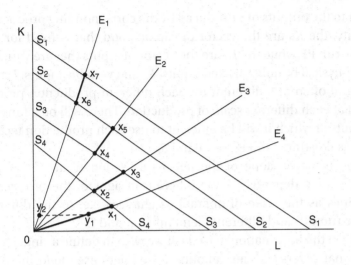

Figure 5 Expansion paths with four different production
technologies

associated with points that are integer multiples of the coordinates
of x_6, and hence all lie on E_1, will increase by the same multiples.
Nothing about replication allows us to assume that there exist
other technologies that will allow those higher and higher outputs
to be produced with technical efficiency (if at all) by radically
different factor combinations, such as much labour and a little
capital.

B5. Type-1 and Type-2 Production Functions

If we wish to study what is happening within the firm at each scale
of its output, there is no disagreement that we need separate short-
run PFs for each production process:

$$y^1 = f_1(\overline{K}_1, L_1); y^2 = f_2(\overline{K}_2, L_2); y^3 = f_3(\overline{K}_3, L_3);$$
$$and\ y^4 = f_4(\overline{K}_4, L_4.) \tag{A-1}$$

where each f_i refers to the production facility that it is optimal to
use when the process of that number is being employed, the y's

refer to the outputs of y produced by the corresponding production facility, the Ks are the vector of capital good that is fixed for any short-run PF while the Ls are the vector of inputs that are variable. The physical bundles of fixed inputs, $\overline{K}$, and variable inputs, L, may be, and often are, different for each different production process used at each different scale of production. There will be a range of outputs at which it will be efficient to use each production technique as illustrated in Figures 4 and 5.

The negative slope of the left-hand section of any U-shaped LRAC curve depends on the different designs of the production facilities as the scale of operations changes, i.e. to the different short-run PFs and different elements in K and L.

Given the information in (A-1), if we wish to define a single type-2 PF that covers all scales of output, we might use the form

$$y = max[f_1(\overline{K}_1, L_1); f_2(\overline{K}_2, L_2); \ldots f_n(\overline{K}_n, L_n)]. \tag{A-2}$$

This will define the most output that can be produced with every possible technically efficient combination of inputs. Once again there will be many input combinations that are technically inefficient and so would never be employed. For some levels of output more than one technique may be technically efficient leaving the choice between them to depend on relative factor prices, while at other levels there may be only one technically efficient technique, leaving the input ratio to be determined by relative prices only if there is room for factor substitution in that production process. It is not obvious, however, how the information given by (A-2) could be compressed into a single PF equation of the sort found in the textbooks in which each input only occurs once and a single function defines all of the technically efficient possibilities that use very different production technologies.

B6. Conclusion

We conclude that the typical textbook representation of the PF has some serious problems. When it contains isoquants that span all, or most, of the input space, it is implicitly assuming that a given level of production can be obtained with technical efficiency using a wide range of input ratios and hence a wide variety of production techniques. This cannot be shown by a single type-1 PF. With a type-2 PF, the requirement is that different production techniques, such as mass and artisan production are both technically efficient for each level of output. Simple observation suggests that there are many levels of output for which both technologies cannot be technically efficient. For example, above a relatively low level of output, capital-intensive mass production techniques technically dominate labour-intensive craft production techniques at all relative input prices. Furthermore, since many products, such as computers and electron microscopes, require complex capital goods for their production, there is no way that they can be produced by much labour and only a few simple tools. At the opposite extreme, until robots become much more efficient than they are today, there are many service products such as haircuts and high-end restaurant meals that cannot be produced by a little labour and an array of complex capital goods. When these impossibilities are taken into account, there is no reason to expect any single isoquant to span anything close to the whole possible range of the input ratios, nor to expect the expansion path for given relative prices to be continuous.

This is not the place to debate how much harm is done by the fiction that the PF typically has the form given it in the textbooks. But surely it is not a bad thing to suggest that students (and their teachers) should be aware of the reality that they are abstracting from when they use the textbook definition of a type-2 PF and that, in some applications, the resulting fictions may be misleading.

Classified References

A. Dictionaries, Encyclopaedias and Introductory Textbooks[1]

Abraham-Frois, G. 2008. 'Average and Marginal Cost'. In William A. Darity Jr., ed., *International Encyclopedia of the Social Sciences* (2nd Edition). Detroit: Macmillan Reference USA.

Ammer, C. and D.S. Ammer. 1984. *Dictionary of Business and Economics* (Revised and Expanded Edition). London: The Free Press.

Bain, J.S. 1968. 'Economies of Scale'. In D.L. Stills, ed., *International Encyclopedia of the Social Sciences*. New York, NY: Gale.

Bannock, G., R. Baxter and R. Davies. 1984. *Penguin Dictionary of Economics* (3rd Edition). Harmondsworth, Middlesex; New York, NY: Penguin Books.

　2003. *Penguin Dictionary of Economics* (7th Edition). London; New York, NY: Penguin Books.

Barbosa-Filho, N.H. 2008. 'Verdoorn's Law'. In William A. Darity Jr., ed., *International Encyclopedia of the Social Sciences* (2nd Edition). Detroit: Macmillan Reference USA.

Baumol, W.J. 2008. 'Indivisibilities'. In S.N. Durlaf and L. Blume, eds., *The New Palgrave Dictionary of Economics* (2nd Edition). New York, NY: Palgrave Macmillan.

Becattinni, G. 2008. 'Internal Economies'. In S.N. Durlaf and L. Blume, eds., *The New Palgrave Dictionary of Economics* (2nd Edition). New York, NY: Palgrave Macmillan.

Becker, G. 1999. 'Pecuniary Economies'. In R.E. McAuliffe, ed., *The Blackwell Encyclopedic Dictionary of Managerial Economics*. Oxford: John Wiley and Sons, Inc.

Black, J., N. Hashimzade and G. Myles. 2012. *A Dictionary of Economics* (4th Edition). Oxford: Oxford University Press.

---

[1] I have grouped introductory texts under A rather than B with the rest of the textbooks because their converge is less formal than the micro texts, and hence more like those in the other categories under A.

Bohm, P. 2008. 'External Economies'. In S.N. Durlaf and L. Blume, eds., *The New Palgrave Dictionary of Economics* (2nd Edition). New York, NY: Palgrave Macmillan.

Brush, B.C. 1994. 'Economies of Scale'. In D. Greenwald, ed., *The Mcgraw-Hill Encyclopedia of Economics* (2nd Edition). New York, NY: McGraw-Hill, Inc.

Calhoun, C. 2002. *Dictionary of the Social Sciences*. Oxford: Oxford University Press.

Carlaw, K. and Richard G. Lipsey. 2008a. 'Returns to Scale'. In William A. Darity Jr., ed., *International Encyclopedia of the Social Sciences* (2nd Edition). Detroit: Macmillan Reference USA.

2008b. 'Returns to Scale, Asymmetric'. In William A Darity Jr., ed., *International Encyclopedia of the Social Sciences* (2nd Edition). Detroit: Macmillan Reference USA.

Case, K.E., R.C. Fair and S.M. Oster. 2012. *Principles of Economics* (10th Edition). New York, NY: Prentice-Hall.

Cowell, F.A. 2006. *Microeconomics: Principles and Analysis*. Oxford: Oxford University Press.

Eatwell, J. 2008. 'Returns to Scale'. In S.N. Durlaf and L. Blume, eds., *The New Palgrave Dictionary of Economics* (2nd Edition). New York, NY: Palgrave Macmillan.

Feiwel, G.R. and I. Feiwel. 1997. 'Production and Cost Functions'. in F.N. Magill, ed., *International Encyclopedia of Economics*. Chicago: Salem Press Inc.

Frank, R.H. 2008. *Microeconomics and Behavior* (7th Edition). New York, NY: McGraw-Hill/Irwin.

Frank, R.H. and B.S. Bernake. 2009. *Principles of Microeconomics* (4th Edition). New York, NY: McGraw-Hill/Irwin.

Farrell, M.J. 1997. 'Economies and Diseconomies of Scale'. In F.N. Magill, ed., *International Encyclopedia of Economics*. Chicago: Salem Press Inc.

Frevert, P. 1997. 'Returns to Scale'. In F.N. Magill, ed., *International Encyclopedia of Economics*. Chicago: Salem Press Inc.

Graaff, J.d.V. 1987. 'Pecuniary and Non-pecuniary Economies'. In J. Eatwell, M. Milgate, and P. Newman, eds., *The New Palgrave Dictionary of Economics* (1st Edition). New York, NY: Palgrave Macmillan.

Gravelle, H. and R. Rees. 1992. *Microeconomics* (2nd Edition). London, UK: Longman.

Henderson, J.M. 1994. 'Production Function'. In D. Greenwald, ed., *The Mcgraw-Hill Encyclopedia of Economics* (2nd Edition). New York, NY: McGraw-Hill, Inc.

Jackson, D. 1996. 'Economies of Scale'. In A. Kuper and J. Kuper, eds., *The Social Science Encyclopedia* (2nd Edition). New York, NY: Routledge.

Jorgenson, D. 2008. 'Production Functions'. In S.N. Durlauf and L.E. Blume eds., *The New Palgrave Dictionary of Economics* (2nd Edition). New York, NY: Palgrave Macmillan.

Krugman, P. and R. Wells. 2009. *Microeconomics* (2nd Edition). New York, NY: Worth Publishers.

Mankiw, N.G. 2006. *Principles of Microeconomics* (4th Edition). Mason, OH: Thomson South-Western.

McAffee, R.P. 2006. *Introduction to Economic Analysis*. Open-source, retrieved from www.mcafee.cc/Introecon/IEA2007.pdf.

McAuliffe, R.E. 1999. 'Production Functions'. In R.E. McAuliffe, ed., *The Blackwell Encyclopedic Dictionary of Managerial Economics*. Oxford: John Wiley and Sons, Inc.

McConnell, C.R., S.L Brue and S.M. Flynn. 2012. *Microeconomics: Principles, Problems, and Policies* (19th Edition). New York, NY: McGraw-Hill Irwin.

Parkin, M., M. Powell and K. Mathews. 2005. *Economics* (6th Edition). Essex: Pearson Education Ltd.

Pass, C., B. Lowes and L. Davies. 2005. *Collins Dictionary of Economics*. London: Collins.

Pearce, D.W. 1992. *The MIT Dictionary of Modern Economics* (4th Edition). Cambridge, MA: MIT Press.

Perloff, J.M. 2012. *Microeconomics* (6th Edition). Boston, MA: Pearson Education Inc.

Pindyck, R.S. and D.L. Rubinfeld. 2009. *Microeconomics* (7th Edition). Upper Saddle River, NJ: Pearson Prentice Hall.

Pratten, C. 2004. 'Economies of Scale'. In Adam Kuper, ed., *Social Science Encyclopedia* (3rd Edition). New York, NY: Routledge.

Rutherford, D. 2000. *Routledge Dictionary of Economics*. Cornwall: TJ International Ltd.

Seldon, A. and F.G. Pennance. 1976. *Everyman's Dictionary of Economics*. London: J.M. Dent & Sons Ltd.

Setterfield, M. 2001. 'Increasing Returns to Scale'. In P. O'Hara, ed., *Encyclopedia of Political Economy*. London; New York, NY: Routledge.

Shim, J.K. and J.G. Siegal. 1995. *Wiley Dictionary of Economics*. Hoboken, NJ: John Wiley & Sons.

Silvestre, J. 1987. 'Economies and Diseconomies of Scale'. In J. Eatwell, M. Milgate and P. Newman, eds., *The New Palgrave Dictionary of Economics* (1st Edition). New York, NY: Palgrave Macmillan.

Sloman, J. 2006. *Economics* (6th Edition). Essex: Pearson Education Ltd.

Smith, V.L. 1968. 'Production'. In D.L. Sills, ed.., *International Encyclopedia of the Social Sciences*. New York, NY: Gale.

Stockfisch, J.A. 1968. 'External Economies and Diseconomies'. In D.L. Sills, ed., *International Encyclopedia of the Social Sciences*. New York, NY: Gale.

Varian, H.R. 1992. *Microeconomic Analysis* (3rd Edition). London; New York, NY: W.W. Norton and Company Inc.

Vassilakas, S. 1987. 'Increasing Returns to Scale'. In J. Eatwell, M. Milgate and P. Newman, eds., *The New Palgrave Dictionary of Economics* (1st Edition). New York, NY: Palgrave Macmillan.

B. Microeconomics Textbooks

Baumol, W.J., 1977. *Economic Theory and Operations Analysis*. Englewood Cliffs, NJ: Prentice Hall.

Binger, B.R. and E. Hoffman. 1988. *Microeconomics with Calculus*. Glenview, IL: Scott, Foresman and Company.

DeSerpa, A.C. 1985. *Microeconomic Theory: Issues and Applications*. Boston: Allyn and Bacon, Inc.

Eaton, B.C., Eaton, D.F. and D.W. Allen. 2012. *Microeconomics: Theory with Applications* (3rd Edition). Toronto: Pearson Canada.

Griffiths, A. and S. Wall. 2000. *Intermediate Microeconomics: Theory and Applications*. Essex: Pearson Education Limited.

Hirshleifer, J., A. Glazer and D. Hirshleifer. 2005. *Price Theory and Applications: Decisions, Markets, and Information* (7th Edition). Cambridge; New York, NY: Cambridge University Press.

Jehle, G.A. and P.J. Reny. 2001. *Advanced Microeconomic Theory* (2nd Edition). New York, NY: Addison Wesley.

Kamerschen, D.R. and L.M. Valentine. 1977. *Intermediate Microeconomic Theory*. Cincinnati, OH: South-Western Publishing Co.

Mahanty, A.K. 1980. *Intermediate Micro-Economics with Applications*. New York, NY: Academic Press.

Mansfield, E. 1979. *Microeconomics: Theory and Applications* (3rd Edition). New York, NY: Norton.

Miller, R.L. 1978. *Intermediate Microeconomics: Theory, Issues, and Applications*. McGraw-Hill Inc.

Nicholson, W. 1979. *Intermediate Microeconomics and Its Applications*. Hinsdale, IL: The Dryden Press.

Quirk, J.P. 1987. *Intermediate Microeconomics*. Chicago: Science Research Associated Inc.

Sher, W. and R. Pinola. 1986. *Modern Microeconomic Theory*. New York, NY: Elsevier Science Publishing Co.

Shone, R. 1981. *Applications in Intermediate Microeconomics*. Oxford: Wiley.

C. Other References

Adams, James. 1991. *Flying Buttresses, Entropy and O-Rings: The World of an Engineer*. Cambridge, MA: Harvard University Press.

Arthur, W. Brian. 1994. *Increasing Returns and Path Dependence in the Economy*. Ann Arbor, MI: University of Michigan Press.

Bain, J.S. 1954. 'Economies of Scale, Concentration, and the Condition of Entry in Twenty Manufacturing Industries'. *The American Economic Review* 44(1): 15–39.

Bain, J.S. 1956. 'Barriers to Competition: Their Character and Consequences in Manufacturing Industries'. Cambridge, MA: Harvard University Press.

Blaug, M. 1978. *Economic Theory in Retrospect* (3rd Edition). Cambridge; New York, NY: Cambridge University Press.

Bobzin, Hagen. 1998. *Indivisibilities: Microeconomic Theory with Respect to Indivisible Goods and Factors*. New York, NY: Physica-Verlag

Cardwell, D.S.L. 1995. *The Norton History of Technology*. New York, NY: Norton.

  1971. *From Watt to Clausius: The Rise of Thermodynamics in the Early Industrial Age*. London: Heinemann.

Chandra, Ramesh and Roger Sandilands. 2006. 'The Role of Pecuniary External Economies and Economies of Scale in the Theory of Increasing Returns', *Review of Political Economy* 18 (2): 193–208.

Chandra, Ramesh and Roger Sandilands. 2009. 'Reply ot Roy Grieve on Increasing Returns'. *Review of Political Economy* 21(4): 655–64.

Carlaw, Kennith I. 2004. 'Uncertainty and Complementarity Lead to Increasing Returns to Durability'. *Journal or Economic Behaviour and Organization* 53(2): 261–82.

Carlaw, Kennith I. and Richard G. Lipsey. 2003. 'Productivity, Technology and Economic Growth: What Is the Relationship?' *Journal of Economic Surveys* 17(3): 457–95.

2004. 'Total Factor Productivity and the Measurement of Technological Change'. *The Canadian Journal of Economics* 31(4): 1118–50.

2011. 'Sustained Endogenous Growth Driven by Structured and Evolving General Purpose Technologies'. *Journal of Evolutionary Economics* 21(4): 563–93.

Chandler Alfred, D. 1990. *Scale and Scope: The Dynamics of Industrial Capitalism*. Cambridge, MA: Belknap Press.

Eaton, B. Curtis and Richard G. Lipsey. 1977. 'The Introduction of Space into the Neo-Classical Model of Value Theory'. In M.J. Artis and A.R. Nobay, eds., *Studies in Modern Economics*. Oxford: Basil Blackwell.

1997. *On the Foundations of Monopolistic Competition and Economic Geography: The Selected Essays of B. Curtis Eaton and Richard G. Lipsey*. Cheltenham: Edward Elgar Publishing.

Grieve, Roy H. 2010. 'Pecuniary External Economies, Economies of Scale and Increasing Returns: A Note of Dissent'. *Review of Political Economy* 22(1): 127–40.

Hirschman, A. 1958. *The Strategy of Economic Development*. New Haven, CT: Yale University Press.

Hiscock, Eric C. 1965. *Cruising Under Sail*. Oxford: Oxford University Press.

Kaldor, N. 1972. 'On the Irrelevance of Equilibrium Economics'. *The Economic Journal* 82(328): 1237–55.

Koopmans, T.C. 1957. *Three Essays on the State of Economic Science*. New York, NY: McGraw Hill.

Krugman, Paul. 'The Fall and Rise of Development Economics'. http://web.mit.edu/krugman/www/dishpan.html.

Lipsey, Richard G. 2009. 'Some Legacies of Robbins' *An Essay on the Nature and Significance of Economic Science*'. *Economica (Special issue Robbins's Essay at 75)* 76(1): 845–56.

Lipsey, Richard G., Kenneth Carlaw and Clifford Bekar, 2005. *Economic Transformations: General Purpose Technologies and Long-Term Economic Growth*. Oxford: Oxford University Press.

Morroni, M. (1992). *Production Process and Technical Change.* Cambridge: Cambridge University Press.

Mokyr, Joel 1990. *The Lever of Riches: Technological Creativity and Economic Progress.* New York, NY: Oxford University Press.

Murphy, R.A., A. Shleifer and R. Vishny. 1989. 'Industrialisation and the Big Push'. *Journal of Political Economy* 97(5): 1003-26.

Romer, Paul. 1990. 'Endogenous Technological Change'. *Journal of Political Economy* 98(5): S71-102.

Rosenberg, Nathan. 1982. *Inside the Black Box: Technology and Economics.* Cambridge: Cambridge University Press.

Rosenberg, Nathan and L.K. Birdzell. 1986. *How the West Grew Rich.* New York, NY: Basic Books.

Viner, Jacob. 1931. 'Cost Curves and Supply Curves'. Reprinted in George Stigler and Kenneth Boulding, eds., *AEA Readings in Price Theory.* London: George Allen and Unwin.

Young, A. Allyn. 1928. 'Increasing Returns and Economic Progress'. *The Economic Journal* 38(152): 527-42.

Printed in the United States
by Baker & Taylor Publisher Services

Printed in the United States
By Bookmasters